TIMELESS TEACHINGS FROM MRS. STROUPE'S BLACKBOARD

Inspirational Wisdom Through the Ages

Compiled & Edited By
DANICA DE LA MORA

Foreword By
NANCY STROUPE MORRISON

MMXX

Timeless Teachings from Mrs. Stroupe's Blackboard:
Inspirational Wisdom Through the Ages

Cover image: Nancy Jones Stroupe c. 1930s
Original material compiled by Nancy Jones Stroupe
Cover design and copy by Danica De La Mora and
        Nancy Stroupe Morrison
Book design and layout by Danica De La Mora
Proofreading by Nancy Stroupe Morrison
Quotes in this book are attributed to the original author when the author is known.

Published by Timeless Treasures Publishing
P.O. Box 278
Crossnore, NC 28616

First edition: October, 2020.

ISBN: 978-1-953940-00-1

Manufactured in the United States of America.

This book is dedicated to my incredible mother,
Nancy Stroupe Morrison,
and to my most wonderful grandparents,
Nancy and Odes Stroupe.

Thank you for the volumes of wisdom you imparted
with your illustrative teachings,
your indefatigable support and encouragement,
your unwavering presence and stability,
your silent and gentle guidance,
your wonderful character,
your loving devotion,
and your continual
connection.

I love you more every day.

Contents

Foreword
by
Nancy Stroupe Morrison

I was a young adult before I fully realized just how fortunate I was that Providence gifted me with Nancy Jones Stroupe for my mother. Somehow I always thought of her as the "Queen of English." It is slightly ironic that I hadn't really taken note of her close resemblance to Queen Elizabeth until one of my friends (also a former student of hers) mentioned it to me. Who knows? Her grandfather came to this country from London. And that is where my preference for hot tea with cream and sugar originated.

As my husband Bruce always said, "Not a day passes when I am in Avery County that I don't hear something about Nancy's extraordinary mother." It has been more than 20 years since my mother's passing, so it is quite an accolade that people continue to praise her!

Growing up in the small North Carolina village of Crossnore in the middle of the Blue Ridge Mountains, I missed some of the opportunities children from larger towns and cities enjoyed. But my large, wonderful family of aunts, uncles, and cousins (Stroupes, Sloops, and Staffords) provided love, lessons in life, and a sense of belongingness and security that more than made up for any shortcomings.

One of the nicest gifts my mother gave me was making sure I heard the correct grammar as I was growing up. She always told me it was easier to learn things correctly the first time than it was to correct them later. Yes, I learned the rules of grammar, but I really didn't need to. I could tell correct grammar just by listening to the phrase or sentence. As I said, I grew up in a small town and our school was also small. It was inevitable that I would have my mother for a teacher. I'm so glad I did. I had her for several years of high school English and two years of Latin and she was easily the best teacher I ever had.

Through the years, in grade and high school, I resented the fact that my mother refused to help me with my homework, especially since other students would call her and she would help them! When I asked her why she would not help me, she told me she wanted to stand up at my graduation and tell everyone that she had never helped me with my homework so no one could accuse her of favoritism or me of having an unfair advantage. She was the senior class homeroom teacher and she did exactly that the night of my graduation from Newland High School!

I've often wondered at the respect my mother commanded in the classroom and the control that seemed so effortless. But in class, she was passionate about her subject and her lessons were always interesting. She loved Greek and Roman mythology and Elizabethan English. She loved the great writers from Chaucer to Shakespeare to Hemmingway to Thurber and she made their stories come alive. Ask anyone in Avery County to recite *The Prologue to the Canterbury Tales*. If they were students of hers, they will start reeling off the opening words, "Whan that Aprille . . . ."

I remember walking into her classroom each day and checking for the day's quote on her blackboard, written in her very unusual writing, which was somehow a combination of writing and printing. We all did. Her quote to start the day was a part of our lives for all those years. She had collected those quotes all her life and it was interesting to see what she chose each day. How fitting it is to honor her contributions with a compilation of those very wise quotes!

At home, she loved to sit by the fireplace and read. She cooked big meals on weekends when my father was home. He traveled for Nationwide Insurance during the week. When he was gone, we had simple meals of sandwiches and soup. Although my mother's family was equally wonderful, they were in South Carolina and we saw them only on special occasions. My mother fit in very well with the Stroupe side of the family and the many aunts, uncles, and cousins looked after us when my father was traveling. And then we all got together on weekends. She loved boating on Lake James, square dancing with friends, playing with the dogs and cats we always had around (yes, strays were welcome!), playing organ and/or singing in the Crossnore Presbyterian Church choir, and writing the church newsletter, "The Cornerstone."

But, most of all, she was a wonderful, warm and loving, fun mother whose leaving this world left a unfillable void in many hearts. Especially mine.

Preface

My grandmother, Nancy Jones Stroupe, was quite a lady. There was never a hair out of place, a sour word out of her mouth, or an unkind thought about anyone unless she kept it to herself. She was always tidy in her appearance. She was warm, kind, agreeable, gentle, feminine, and patient. She was proficient in commanding when necessary, but she always lovingly deferred to my grandfather in his presence. They were complimentarily different, like two halves of a whole, and together they represented the ideal of the home and the community. She was a perfect example of the timeless lady every woman should strive to be, regardless of epoch.

I appreciate that my grandparents were so involved in my life. They never missed an event I had at school, and I always knew that no matter where they were, on a journey or at their other home, they would magically appear whenever there was a special occasion. Their desires varied enough that no matter what I wished to do, at least one of them would likely accompany me. Evenings with them were delightful and cozy. We were usually doing something and our activities often were sprinkled with nuts and candy. Yes, childhood was a happy time!

During the quiet moments, I would often find her sitting by the lamp and fireplace, in that soft, warm chair, reading a book or working on a crossword puzzle. Often I would crawl onto her lap and she would lay down whatever previously had her attention and pick up a book that I would enjoy. Together we would embark on an exciting adventure. Life was always about learning and personal development. I never doubted their love for a moment, nor did I tire of it. If only everyone could be fortunate enough to have loving grandparents with such devotion, stability, and support.

Recently I stumbled onto an overstuffed notebook that she saved from her years of teaching. Although dusty and musty, the appearance and smell could not conceal the multitude of wisdom and humor contained within. I decided that it would be an entertaining book for a coffee table in any home. Because her presence is still missed by many, I wanted to compile a collection particularly for the students she so loved, especially now that they are old enough to understand some of them, but also to create a book that people everywhere could enjoy.

After all of the years without my special grandparents, now I can return to that cozy chair by the fireplace with this book in hand, near my wonderful mother, and imagine the room filled again with their love and laughter. As we remember the fun times and revisit the maxims my grandmother enjoyed, it will be almost as wonderful as it used to be.

As a tribute to that spectacular lady with brilliance and lovely feminine essence, I now present to you her cut-and-paste collection of wisdom and amusement. It is my hope that you will be amused and enlightened as well.

All the best to you,

Danica De La Mora
September 30, 2020

Advice

❖ Advice is like snow; the softer it falls, the longer it dwells upon and the deeper it sinks into the mud. – *Samuel T. Coleridge*

❖ You cannot expect to live in a sunny world if you are wearing a cloud on your brow.

❖ Courtesy costs nothing, yet it buys things that are priceless.

❖ When a man thinks he is important, he should ask what the world would miss if he were gone.

❖ The best way to make a fire with two sticks is to make sure that one of them is a match.

❖ The best place to find a helping hand is at the end of your arm.

❖ He who sets a bad example never knows what will hatch.

❖ Live for yourself alone and you become smaller; live for others and you grow greater.

❖ To be popular, give a minimum of advice and a maximum of applause.

❖ When you can, use discretion; when you can't, use a club.

❖ Take care of the common sense and your worries will take care of themselves.

❖ A poor excuse is better than none—if it works.

❖ Second thoughts are best—if they are less expensive.

❖ The man who can control his feet and his tongue will keep out of a lot of wrong places.

❖ Don't place yourself on a pedestal; you might be called down.

❖ The book I will buy if I find it, and not relegate to the shelf, is one that gives simple directions—on how *not* to do it myself. – *S. Omar Barker*

❖ Advice is what you take for a cold. – *Thomas J. O'Brien*

❖ You'll never get indigestion from swallowing your pride occasionally.

❖ Be tolerant of that which is no business of yours; sometimes it may be yours. – *Chronicle, Seville, Ohio*

❖ Don't be a knocker. You can't saw wood with a hammer.

❖ If you want a pat on the back, let the other fellow do it.

❖ If you find your life empty, try putting more into it. – *K-Lens-M Komments*

❖ Despite inflation, a penny for most people's thoughts is still a fair price. – *Sol Broad*

❖ When all is said and done, it's best to leave it that way.

❖ The best way to make a long story short is to skip it.

Advice

❖ Don't buy it for a song unless you're sure what the pitch is.

❖ Always look for quality. It will be remembered long after the price has been forgotten.

❖ Push the community wagon along; don't ride and drag your feet.

❖ If the times don't fit you, fit yourself to the times.
  – *K-Lens-M Komments* (August, 1964)

❖ The man hasn't been born yet who doesn't feel a little flattered when somebody takes his advice.

❖ You might as well keep your mouth shut. If you talk about yourself you're a bore. If you talk about others, you're a gossip.

❖ Compare yourself not with others, but with what you might be.

❖ Don't put on too many airs as you float down life's stream; your boat may strike a snag.

❖ If your foot slips, you can always recover your balance; if your tongue slips, you can never recover your words.

❖ A good start for the New Year is to out-fumble the other guy for the check. – *K-Lens-M Komments*

❖ To take a great weight off your mind, discard your halo.

❖ If you have done something good, forget it and do something better.

❖ Hear no evil, see no evil, speak no evil—and you will never be a success at a bridge party.

❖ Never mistake difficulties for impossibilities.

❖ Bad news and bad eggs should always be broken gently.

❖ If you must gossip, do so with your ears open and your mouth closed.

❖ Don't look at the world through morose-colored glasses.
  – *K-Lens-M Komments* (March, 1964)

❖ The great secret is not having bad manners or good manners or any other particular sort of manners, but having the same manner for all human souls; in short, behaving as if you were in Heaven, where there are no third-class carriages, and one soul is as good as another. – *George Bernard Shaw*

❖ If you can tell the difference between good advice and bad advice, you don't need advice. – *Roger Devlin*

❖ Say nothing if you have nothing to say. Fast thinkers are more successful than fast talkers.

❖ When in doubt as to what to do today, ask yourself what you will wish you had done when tomorrow comes.

❖ He who considers consequences is able to control causes.

❖ People who ask for advice are usually seeking sympathy.

❖ Having a way of your own keeps you out of the way of others.

❖ He is a wise man who knows what not to say, provided he doesn't say it.

❖ Have reasons for your actions and you won't need excuses.

❖ Don't call the world dirty just because you have forgotten to clean your glasses.

Advice

❖ An ounce of keeping one's mouth shut is worth a pound of explanation.

❖ It's always a good idea to keep your words soft and sweet, because you never know when you'll have to eat them.

❖ Never meet trouble halfway—it will gladly make the full trip.
  – *K-Lens-M Komments* (September, 1963)

❖ Don't judge your future by your past; you may be discouraged.

❖ So live that you need not be afraid of tomorrow or ashamed of yesterday.

❖ He who doesn't do right should always expect to get left.

❖ Don't worry about finding your station in life. Someone is sure to tell you where to get off.

❖ Risk but little on the opinion of a man who has nothing to lose.

❖ It is folly to explain or complain. – *K-Lens-M Komments*

❖ Trust people with your money, but never with your reputation.

❖ Forget your past troubles, and be ready for the new ones that are coming.

❖ A good scare is worth more to a man than good advice.
  – *E. W. Howe*

❖ So live that you are known for your deeds, not your mortgages.

❖ It is never safe to be nostalgic about something until you're absolutely certain there's no chance of its coming back.
  – *Bill Vaughan, Bell Syndicate*

❖ Whenever you find the bait of something for nothing, look for the trap. – *Arnold Glasgow*

❖ To get to the top, go to the bottom of things.

❖ Watch your step; the neighbors will watch your misstep.

❖ Never discourage another's plans unless you have something better to offer.

❖ Count your blessings and faultfinding will fade away.

❖ If you are sure you are right, let the other fellow find it out at his leisure.

❖ Cooperate with your conscience. You'll live a more comfortable life.

❖ Never take advice from a stranger and ignore that of your own conscience.

❖ To avoid trouble, breathe through the nose. It keeps the mouth shut. – *(September, 1960 – Carolina Co-operation)*

❖ It's no use to turn over a new leaf unless you plan to use a little moral mucilage.

❖ Staying out of expensive dives will permit you to keep your head above water.

❖ Don't find fault—find a remedy. Anybody can complain. – *Henry Ford*

❖ Keep your fears to yourself, but share your courage with others. – *Robert Louis Stevenson*

❖ In order to stay on the square, be careful with whom you make the rounds.

❖ It is necessary to cultivate good habits. The bad ones grow wild.

❖ Anything that causes trouble costs too much.

❖ Better have a care about throwing your weight around; somebody may be holding a pitchfork.

❖ Before you criticize those who are bad, make sure you are good enough to do it.

❖ Given the choice, take one bad beating rather than a series of little ones.

❖ When things go wrong, don't go with them.

❖ The world's shortest sermon: "When in doubt, don't."
 – Milwaukee Journal

❖ Advice is like castor oil—easy enough to give up, rather uneasy to take.

❖ Don't look a gift compliment in the mouth.
 – K-Lens-M Komments

❖ Let everyone sweep in front of his own door, and the whole world will be clean. *– Goethe*

❖ Drift with the tide and eventually you'll land on the rocks.

❖ Never borrow trouble. You'll always have much more of it dropped in your lap than you can conveniently handle.

❖ To keep people from jumping down your throat—keep your mouth shut.

❖ The only gracious way to accept an insult is to ignore it; if you can't ignore it, top it; if you can't top it, laugh at it; if you can't laugh at it, it's probably deserved. – *Russell Lynes*

❖ Don't forget that today is the tomorrow you expected so much of yesterday.

❖ Don't be just yourself with other people. Try always to be your better self.

❖ When you are tempted to tell your troubles to other people, remember that half of them are not interested, and the other half are glad that you are finally getting what's coming to you.

❖ Pleasant memories must be arranged for in advance.

❖ Never laugh at the fallen; there may be slippery places in your own path.

❖ To save face, keep the lower half shut.

❖ Always look ahead and prepare, rather than look back and regret.

❖ Bend your knees, not your elbows, if you expect to solve your problems.

❖ How to say "no" in eight words: "I'll think it over and let you know."

❖ If you long for the good old days, try reading this by the light of an old oil lamp.

❖ The man who lends free advice is actually borrowing trouble.

❖ It is usually a waste of time to tell a man something for his own good.

❖ Laugh a little more at your troubles and your neighbors will respect you for it.

❖ Before you ask for advice, explore your own head; there may be something in it.

❖ If you can read the handwriting on the wall, it was not written by the average adult.

❖ Ask advice, but use your own common sense.

❖ Be easygoing, but it never pays to slow down to a standstill.

❖ When people ask you for your candid opinion, they usually expect it to be complimentary.

❖ The easiest way to distinguish between young plants and weeds is to pull up everything. If they come up again they are weeds.

❖ If you look like your passport photo, you need the trip.
   – *Edward Arnold*

❖ Better than counting your years is to make all your years count.

❖ He who waits for something to turn up had better keep his eyes pointed toward his toes.

❖ Not much difference between keeping your chin up and sticking your neck out, but it's worth knowing.

❖ What a big difference there is between giving advice and lending a hand.

❖ Never call yourself a fool. Your friends may suspect you have inside information.

❖ Don't get carried away on a wave of enthusiasm. Too many have to row back.

❖ Better be with a few who are right than with many who are wrong.

❖ Don't spend all your time trying to stop something—start something.

❖ When something defies description, let it. – *K-Lens-M Komments*

❖ Be careful when you pass out advice—some people might be foolish enough to follow it.

❖ Have faith in mankind, but it still pays to count your change.

❖ Sometimes the best way to convince a man he is wrong is to let him have his own way.

❖ Don't throw away the old bucket until you know whether the new one holds water.

❖ You save a lot of unnecessary conversation if you remember that people aren't going to take your advice unless you are a lawyer or a doctor and charge them for it. – *Anonymous*

❖ Coasting, remember, also can mean you are going downhill.

❖ The best thing to do for spring fever is absolutely nothing.

Advice

❖ Rest on your laurels and you may be rudely awakened.
– *K-Lens-M Komments* (August, 1963)

❖ Don't get so interested in what you are going to do tomorrow that you don't do anything today.

❖ When you make a mountain out of a molehill, don't expect anyone to climb up to admire the view.

❖ Be sure you are right—hesitate and you are left.

❖ Habit is a cable; we weave a thread of it each day, and it becomes so strong that we cannot break it.

❖ Beware of the fellow who tries to soft soap you. Fish bait is always used to cover a hook.

❖ Don't be one of those husbands who go home and find fault with dinner. Take your wife to a restaurant, where you both can find fault.

❖ The best way to get your name in the newspaper is to walk across the street reading one.

❖ Don't follow the crowd if you expect to be a leader.

❖ If you don't think you are getting what you deserve, go out in the woods and tackle a hornets' nest.

❖ Fools need advice most, but wise men only are better for it.

❖ Sometimes it is really better to fool with a bee than to be with a fool.

❖ It's a waste of time to explain your actions. People prefer to draw their own conclusions.

❖ Take your troubles to the pawnshop and then lose the ticket.

❖ Realization that it is time to get up is the best cure for insomnia.

❖ If you wish to be popular, hand the other fellow a helping hand instead of handing him advice.

❖ One of the hardest things in this world to do is to admit you are wrong. And nothing is more helpful in resolving a situation than its frank admission. – *Disraeli*

❖ Taking things as they come doesn't wear you out as fast as dodging them.

Aging Gracefully

❖ By the time some people realize that time is golden, they are too old to open a savings account.

❖ They call it middle age because that's where it shows the most.

❖ You are young only once, but if you work it right, once is enough.

❖ Life doesn't begin at 40 for those who went like 60 when they were 20. – *Tennessee Ernie Ford*

❖ Brother, you have really reached middle age when you fall asleep resisting temptation.

❖ Do winters keep getting colder or is it just us getting older? – *K-Lens-M Komments*

❖ An adult is one who has stopped growing – except in the middle.

❖ Old men love to give advice. It consoles them for being no longer able to set a bad example.

❖ Middle age is that time of life when you don't care where your wife goes, just so you don't have to go along.

❖ When a person has no more illusions, he is suffering from old age.

❖ Middle age is when you feel on Saturday night the way you used to feel on Monday morning.

❖ Middle age: when your figure forgets how to subtract. – *K-Lens-M Komments* (October, 1965)

❖ Life not only begins at 40—that's also when it begins to show. – *Red Skelton*

❖ Middle age is when your narrow waist and broad mind begin to change places. – *Ben Klizner*

❖ An old-timer is a fellow who has just made the last payment on his home.

❖ The young live in the future, the old in the past, leaving only a few to live in the present.

❖ An octogenarian was asked if he had his life to live over, would he make the same mistakes. "Yes," he replied, "but I would start sooner."

❖ Never could understand why life's problems don't hit us when we are 18 and know everything.

❖ Many people are rapidly approaching the "metallic age"—gold in their teeth, silver in their hair and lead in their pants.

❖ The best thing about getting old is that all those things you couldn't have when you were young you no longer want. – L. S. McCandless

❖ Middle age: when you look forward to a dull evening. – *Joe Ryan*

❖ The boy whose dad used to drop him off at school and then drive on to work now has a son who drops him off at work and then drives on to school.

❖ When a man is too old to act young, and too young to act old, he should act like a grown-up.

❖ Old age is when you find yourself using one bend-over to pick up two things.

❖ A man is getting old when he inspects the food instead of the waitress.

❖ A man is aging when he scans the menu before the waitress.
 – *Graphic*

❖ We wonder if it is true that people have candles on birthday cakes just to make light of their age.

❖ Middle age is when your memory is shorter, your experience longer, your stamina lower and your forehead higher.

❖ Awkward age: when you are old enough to know better but don't.
 – *K-Lens-M Komments* (September, 1963)

❖ By the time a man gets old enough to watch his step, he's too old to go anywhere.

❖ The older a man gets, the more he feels that he gets less for his money each time he goes to the barber shop.

❖ The present generation isn't more wicked than any other age. It just fails to pull down the shades.

❖ Many folks are poor and unhappy until they are forty—then they get used to it.

❖ With both girls and autos, the paint conceals the years but the lines give them away.

❖ Retirement is when you finally have the time and money to do the things you no longer want to do.

❖ A noted statistician tells us that at the age of 75 there are 18 percent more women than men. At 75, who cares?

❖ Middle age is that time of life when you no longer need a pillow to play Santa Claus.

❖ Children are not only a comfort to parents in their old age; they help them get there faster.

❖ There's no fool like an old fool. If you don't believe it, ask any young fool.

❖ You have reached middle age when everything the young people do makes you tired.

❖ If the first hundred years are the hardest, why don't things become a bit easier as we grow older? – *K-Lens-M Komments* (April, 1964)

❖ Middle age is that perplexing time of life when we hear two voices calling us, one saying, "Why not?" and the other, "Why bother?" – *Sydney J. Harris*

❖ You grow up the day you have the first real laugh—at yourself.

❖ More people might live to a ripe old age if they weren't so busy providing for it. – *General Features Corp.*

❖ Middle age is when you have more weak days.

❖ Nowadays everything is wrinkle resistant but people.

❖ A neighbor told me, "It's terrible to grow old alone—my wife hasn't had a birthday in seven years."

Aging Gracefully

❖ Middle age is that span of life when you want to show how long your car will last instead of how fast it will go.

❖ When you hit 70, you eat better, sleep sounder, and feel more alive than when you were 30. Obviously it's healthier to have women on your mind than on your knees. – *Maurice Chevalier*

❖ It would be much worse to be born old and have to look forward to growing young and silly.

❖ Middle age is that time of life when women won't tell their age— and men won't act theirs.

❖ I used to dread getting older because I thought I would not be able to do all the things I wanted to do, but now that I am older, I find that I don't want to do them.
— *Lady Astor, on her 80ᵗʰ birthday*

❖ By the time one is rich enough to sleep late, he is so old he always wakes up early.

❖ Middle age: when a daily dozen is followed by several days of daily doesn't. – *Dan Bennett*

❖ Old age never begins until regrets take the place of dreams.

❖ There are better ways of staying young than by acting childish.

❖ You are young only once but you can stay immature indefinitely.

❖ Most of us don't think we're middle-aged until we're not.
— *K-Lens-M Komments* (March, 1964)

❖ Discretion is what comes to a man when he is too old for it to do him any good.

❖ If you want to cure your wife of nervousness, tell her that it's caused by advancing age.

❖ If medical science continues to find ways to prolong life, some of us may actually pay off all the mortgages on our homes.

❖ Being young is a fault that improves daily.

❖ Nowadays the thing to put aside for one's old age is all thought of retirement. – *Edmund J. Kiefer*

❖ Middle age: the period in life when your children leave you one by one, only to return two by two. – *Evan Esar*

❖ The identification of old age with growing old must be avoided. Growing old is an emotion which comes over us at almost any age. I had it myself between the ages of 25 and 30. – *E. M. Forster*

❖ Old age is like everything else. To make a success of it, you've got to start young. – *Felix Martin*

❖ When you're pushing sixty, that's really enough exercise.

❖ Middle age is that time of life when you can do as much as you ever could, but would rather not.

❖ Top-grade statisticians tell us that the average man lives thirty years longer than he did back in 1800. He has to in order to get his taxes paid.

❖ A bad memory today is really an asset. It permits you to enjoy an old movie on television without realizing you saw it years ago.

❖ The older one gets, the harder it is to make ends meet—fingers and toes especially. – *George Hart*

❖ You begin to feel your age when you realize that the beautiful blonde looking your way is giving your son the once over.

❖ When you're young enough or old enough to know everything, nobody listens. – *Arnold H. Glasgow*

❖ By the time a fellow can afford to buy one of those little sports cars, he's too fat and stiff to get into one.

❖ If you want to stay young, associate with young people. If you want to get old in a hurry, just try to keep up with them.

❖ The word obituary has been described as thus: the nice things said about you that you won't get to read.

❖ Age is no obstacle for the fellow who plans for the future.

❖ As a man grows older and wiser, he talks less and says more.

❖ It takes a baby about two years to learn to talk, and about sixty or seventy-five years to learn to keep his mouth shut.

❖ Old-timer: one who recalls when radioactivity was mostly static. – *The Tip*

❖ Middle age is when you have a choice of two temptations and choose the one that will get you home earlier. – *Dan Bennett*

❖ A diplomat is a person who remembers a woman's birthday, but forgets her age.

❖ Old age has some benefits. For instance, you can whistle as you wash your teeth.

❖ It's hard to know exactly where one generation ends and the next

one begins. But it's somewhere around nine o'clock at night.
– *Charles Ruffing in Family Weekly.*

❖ The best thing to save for old age is yourself. – *L. S. McCandless*

❖ An old-timer is one who remembers when "wonder drugs" were mustard plasters and castor oil.

❖ The hardest decision for a woman to make is when to start middle age. – *Warren Hull*

❖ Some women are very loyal—when they reach an age they like, they stick with it.

❖ At a class reunion, you see that most people your own age are a lot older than you are. – *Kathryn Gelander*

❖ You've reached middle age when all you exercise is caution. – *Franklin P. Jones*

❖ Your childhood was quite a few years ago if you think of blackboards as black and Christmas trees as green. – *Bill Vaughan*

❖ It is a myth that the good die young. They sometimes live long enough to get over being good.

❖ An old-timer is one who remembers when a bureau was considered a piece of furniture. – *Carey Williams*

❖ You've reached middle age, brother, when the girl who smiles at you thinks you're one of her father's friends.

❖ We never get too old to learn some new way to be stupid.

The Seven Ages of Woman:
The infant
The little girl
The miss
The young woman
The young woman
The young woman
The young woman

Animals

❖ The older a lamb grows, the more sheepish he becomes.

❖ The stinger of a bee is only .03125 of an inch long. The rest of the twelve inches is pure imagination.

❖ Horse sense is something that a horse has that keeps him from betting on people.

❖ At least the bird in the hand never sings so delightfully as the one in the bush.

❖ Think how a mother kangaroo must feel on a rainy day when the kids can't play outside.

❖ Mosquito: the original skin diver. – *Robert Larr*

❖ The jawbone of an ass is just about as dangerous today as it was in Samson's time.

❖ A bee without a sting makes no honey.

❖ In one respect, men are like horses. They cannot kick and go forward at the same time.

❖ At pony farm: "Compact Horses." – *The Wall Street Journal*

❖ If science finds nothing impossible, let's develop vegetarian mosquitoes. – *K-Lens-M Komments* (August, 1964)

❖ Nature is amazing. Who would have thought of growing a fly swatter on the rear end of a cow?

❖ A local farmer was describing a scarecrow he was using. Pointing out its effectiveness, he said the crows are now bringing back the corn they had stolen last week.

❖ Ad on billboard: "Lion tamer seeks tamer lion."
  – *K-Lens-M Komments* (May, 1965)

❖ In window of pet shop: "Chock Full O' Mutts." – *Louis Sobol*

❖ Perhaps the bees hum because they don't know the words.
  – *K-Lens-M Komments*

❖ The fact that an owl can't talk may have something to do with his reputation for wisdom.

❖ If you love honey, fear not the bees. – *French proverb*

❖ Horse sense is just stable thinking.

❖ A bird in the hand is said to be worth two in the bush, but that isn't what the birds think.

❖ Porcupine: portable cactus. – *K-Lens-M Komments* (March, 1964)

❖ A peacock has too little in its head and too much in its tail.

❖ I've often wondered why Noah didn't swat the two flies when he had a chance.

❖ Scratch a dog and you'll find a permanent job. – *Franklin P. Jones*

❖ Mosquito: a small insect designed by God to make us think better of flies.

❖ God gives birds their food, but they must fly for it.

❖ A female mosquito lays 1,000,000,000,000,000,000,000 eggs. What an untapped field for birth control! – *K-Lens-M Komments* (May, 1965)

❖ We heard recently that all creatures went into Noah's ark in pairs, except worms—they went aboard in apples.

❖ Night owl: a guy who gets out on a limb. – *K-Lens-M Komments*

❖ A cat that is locked up may change into a lion.

❖ You can't change the nature of a pig by giving him a seat in the parlor.

❖ A little boy was patting a purring kitten and said, "He must be talking to someone; I can hear the busy signal."

❖ Two ducks were walking. One said to the other, "Why don't you stop trying to walk like a woman wearing slacks?"

❖ We have often wondered whether a frog hops to sit down or sits down to hop.

❖ A neighbor tells us that he calls his little hound a watchdog because he is full of ticks.

❖ Notice on a small birdhouse in Darien, Connecticut: "For wrent." – *Jack Armstrong*

❖ Said one caterpillar to another, as they watched a butterfly: "You'll never get me up in one of those things."

Out on a Limerick by Bennett Cerf

A cat in despondency sighed
And resolved to commit suicide.
She passed under the wheels
Of eight automobiles
And under the ninth one she died.
— *Unknown*

Surprising Facts by K-Lens-M Komments

✓ French poodles are exceptionally smart.
✓ Dogs don't have strong vision.
✓ Dogs can distinguish between musical notes a quarter note apart.
✓ The Chihuahua was first developed in Mexico.
✓ The dingo is a wild dog.
✓ It is spelled Pekingese.
✓ The dog is the oldest of all domesticated animals.
✓ Male hippopotami are hen-pecked. (June, 1962)
✓ Bears have sunglass eyelids. (Sept., 1963)
✓ Four fireflies shed enough light for reading. (October, 1963)
✓ Turtles move at a speed of about .01 mile per hour. (March, 1964)
✓ Animals can become dope fiends. (March, 1964)
✓ An elephant's trunk is so sensitive it can pick up a pin. (March, 1964)
✓ Bees may travel 50,000 miles to make a pound of honey. (April, 1964)
✓ Most circus animals are female. (April, 1964)
✓ Porpoises can jump 15 feet in the air. (May, 1964)
✓ The whale strikes the fiercest blow of any animal. (July, 1964)
✓ There are more varieties of land animals than sea animals. (July, 1964)
✓ Walruses keep harems. (July, 1964)
✓ Salmon climb ladders. (July, 1964)
✓ Not all fish lay eggs. (July, 1964)
✓ Fish have no eyelids. (July, 1964)

- ✓ Barnacles are not plant life. (July, 1964)
- ✓ Starfish are luminescent. (July, 1964)
- ✓ A young spider builds a perfect web the first time he tries and with no instructions. (August, 1964)
- ✓ Dogs can hear a watch tick 40 feet away. (August, 1964)
- ✓ The electric eel can kill a horse at 20 feet. (May, 1965)
- ✓ The blue whale far exceeds in size any known creature that has ever existed. (May, 1965)
- ✓ Whooping cranes can be heard from two miles away. (May, 1965)
- ✓ Elephants use a form of penicillin to heal wounds. (May, 1965)
- ✓ Pelicans are almost voiceless. (October, 1965)
- ✓ The strange power to charm reptiles is believed to be hereditary. (October, 1965)

Arts & Entertainment

❖ Accordionist: one who plays both ends against the middle.
— *The Wall Street Journal*

❖ We have noticed that entertainers no longer seem to show evidence of stage fright. The high price of eggs could be the answer.

❖ Genius sprints—but talent generally wins in the long run.

❖ A good storyteller is a person who has a good memory and hopes other people haven't.

❖ Connie Towers tells of being a guest where "there were so many celebrities that I was the only one in the room I'd never heard of."
— *Alex Barris*

❖ Use what talents you have. The woods would be very silent if no birds sang there except those who sing best.

❖ Three things cannot be taught—generosity, poetry and a singing voice. — *Irish Proverb*

❖ Many a starlet has made it to the top because her clothes didn't.
— *Playboy*

❖ Of all the words announcers wheeze, the saddest, barring none, are these: "But first…" — *Margaret Read*

❖ The fellow who is married to his art sometimes feels like suing her for non-support.

❖ Drive-in theater advertises a tear-jerker: "Be sure to bring your windshield wiper." – *Post-Gazette*

❖ A popular song is one that makes us all think we can sing. – *Brick Bits*

❖ Gardeners and film writers dig up the same old plots. – *K-Lens-M Komments* (May, 1965)

❖ Originality: the art of remembering what you hear and forgetting where you heard it. – *Hon. Tommy Douglas*

❖ After hearing the ten top tunes, it is painful to try to imagine what the ten bottom ones would sound like.

❖ You heard that vaudeville died; well, television is the box they put it in. – *Bob Hope*

❖ There are three kinds of people in the world: those who can't stand Picasso, those who can't stand Raphael and those who've never heard of either of them. – *John White in lecture at the Metropolitan Museum of Art, New York*

❖ The symphony of life becomes tiresome when it's too full of rests. – *K-Lens-M Komments* (July, 1964)

❖ Dizzy Dean to a fan who wanted to take his picture, "I'm at your exposal."

❖ Spectacular: a word invented by a network vice-president meaning, "Let's make the show long and more expensive and maybe they won't notice how lousy it is." – *Milton Berle*

❖ Nothing kills a popular tune like playing and singing it. – *K-Lens-M Komments* (May, 1965)

❖ Silent Film: nobody in the audience bought popcorn.
 – *Jimmy Nelson*

❖ Actor: a man with an infinite capacity for taking praise.
 – *Michael Redgrave*

❖ Television: a medium of entertainment that permits a female singer wide range—from high C to low V. – *Evan Esar*

❖ You don't need the subtitles in foreign films to know what's going on. – *K-Lens-M Komments*

❖ Many a man who would like to be a musician has to be content with playing second fiddle at home.

❖ Rock 'n' Roll: a fate worse than deaf. – *Dick White*

❖ An ounce of performance is worth several tons of guesswork.

❖ A stage is what many a teenage girl thinks she should be on, when actually it's just something she's going through.
 – *Barbara Schaeffer*

❖ The real tragedy of life is not being limited to one talent, but failing to use that talent.

❖ We used to have actresses trying to become stars; now we have stars trying to become actresses. – *Sir Laurence Olivier*

❖ One for the money—two for the show—ten for the baby sitter.
 – *K-Lens-M Komments* (September, 1961)

❖ "Sweet Adeline" sounds better when all the basses are loaded.
 – *Wisconsin Herald*

❖ Some of the films shown on TV are too old to stay up that late.

❖ Modern art: oodles of doodles. – *Lawrence Braun*

❖ About all we remember from ancient history is that a pharaoh could maintain a good-sized empire on what it costs to make the movie about it today. – *Bill Vaughan*

❖ Sudden fame is a short-lived flame. – *K-Lens-M Komments* (October, 1963)

❖ I'm an ordinary sort of fellow—42 around the chest, 42 around the waist, 96 around the golf course, and a nuisance around the house. – *Groucho Marx*

❖ Good music is the kind we enjoyed when we were children. Bad music is the kind our kids like. – *William H. Lawrence*

❖ I've often wondered if the men sitting in the bald-headed row bought their tickets from scalpers.

❖ Some amateur actors suffer from hambition. – *K-Lens-M Komments* (August, 1965)

❖ Hollywood publicity: a story about some well-known person doing something he didn't somewhere he wasn't. – *Jimmy Starr*

❖ Crick: Noise made by a Japanese camera. – *Jack Sterling*

❖ Some promising musicians should promise never to play again. – *K-Lens-M Komments* (August, 1963)

❖ As inseparable as ham and ego. – *Chuchu Marinez*

❖ In Europe, all TV programs received from this continent will automatically be Western. – *Harold Coffin*

❖ An actor is a man who tries to be everybody but himself.

❖ Dina Merrill explains the difference between posing for fashion magazines and for Hollywood studio photographers: "In the fashion pictures, you pull in your chest and stick out your hips." – *Dick Williams*

Surprising Facts by K-Lens-M Komments

✓ America has about 39,000,000 amateur photographers. (June, 1962)
✓ Opera originated in Italy. (August, 1963)
✓ Mozart was a child prodigy. (August, 1963)
✓ Tympani are kettledrums. (August, 1963)
✓ Fortissimo means loud. (August, 1963)
✓ An octave is eight notes. (August, 1963)
✓ The piccolo is scaled highest. (August, 1963)
✓ "My Fair Lady" movie rights brought $5,000,000. (August, 1964)
✓ The "Beatles" made history with the most firsts in recording history. (August, 1964)
✓ Colored films go back to about 1909. (May, 1965)
✓ France pioneered newsreels. (May, 1965)

Character & Reputation

- ❖ Character is much easier kept than recovered.

- ❖ It is generally a chain of circumstances that shows up the weak link in a man's character.

- ❖ Character is determined by the things to which a man can say "No."

- ❖ A pessimist is a person who resents the fact that the world was made without seeking his advice.

- ❖ Most hardheads have a crack somewhere. – *K-Lens-M Komments* (October, 1965)

- ❖ The only thing that can keep on growing without nourishment is an ego.

- ❖ Artistic temperament is seldom recognized until it is too old to spank.

- ❖ People who are habitually crooked never know which way to turn.

- ❖ Should you meet a man with a dual personality, tell him to go chase himself.

- ❖ Too many people are interested in making headlines than in making headway.

- ❖ Every man has a chance to improve himself, but some just don't believe in taking chances.

❖ People who take your part usually expect to claim it later as their own.

❖ If you've never heard a good word about some people, it's because you've never heard them talk about themselves.

❖ Every hard-boiled egg is yellow inside.

❖ Conscience is the world's greatest disturber of peace when it wakes up.

❖ There are too many people who reach for the stool when there is a piano to be moved.

❖ The difference between pride and self-respect is that the latter doesn't consider it necessary to strut.

❖ A grouch is a man who thinks the whole world is against him— and how right he is.

❖ By showing up the faults of others, you put your own on display.

❖ The only thing you can get free in this world is criticism.

❖ Telling a man what you think of him isn't worth what it costs.

❖ The average man is one who thinks he isn't.

❖ All of a man's opinions may change except the one he has of himself.

❖ Heat travels faster than cold; you can catch cold easier.

❖ There are two reasons why we don't trust some people. One is because we don't know them, and the other is because we do.

❖ Kleptomania is not catching—it is taking.

❖ Some folks are most trying when they aren't trying.

❖ A man's strength should never be judged by the number of promises he makes.

❖ The sum of a man's intentions usually equals his true character.

❖ A man should be like tea—his real strength appearing when he gets into hot water.

❖ People who are inclined to make light of themselves shouldn't expect others to shine up to them.

❖ Most people have sense enough to mind their own business, but few are willing to let it go at that.

❖ It is amazing how much speed some people pick up when they are backing away from responsibilities.

❖ Most of our suspicions of others are aroused by our knowledge of ourselves. – *Raymond Massey*

❖ The human body is a wonderful thing. Pat a man on the back and he gets a swelled head.

❖ Few headaches are caused by growing pains. – *K-Lens-M Komments* (September, 1961)

❖ Any man who can induce others to think as much of him as he does himself is truly a genius.

❖ Clean your finger before you point at another's spots.

❖ Conceit is God's gift to little men.

❖ The very best men stand in need of pardon.

❖ Braggart: one who enters a conversation feat first.

❖ Staring up to admire your halo creates a pain in the neck.

❖ Stubbornness: petrified stupidity. – *K-Lens-M Komments* (May, 1964)

❖ He who constantly thinks of himself gets mighty little thought from others.

❖ Character is like a tree and reputation like its shadow. The shadow is what we think of it; the tree is the real thing.

❖ An egotist is a conceited ass who thinks he knows as much as you do.

❖ Conceit is a form of "I" strain that doctors cannot cure.

❖ Some folks who live it up discover they have a lot to live down.

❖ Stop bragging about yourself and see if anyone else brings up the subject.

❖ No one can give a good reason for making disagreeable remarks about another.

❖ Misplaced confidence is never found again. – *K-Lens-M Komments* (March, 1964)

❖ He who has nothing but virtues is not much better than he who has nothing but faults.

❖ Honesty has never had to crowd anybody out in order to make a decent living.

❖ A man can mend his ways, but it's difficult to do so the patches won't show.

❖ Few magnifying glasses are powerful enough to enable a man to see his own faults.

❖ Men who have talent for criticism fail to use it on themselves.

❖ Human nature is harder to change than a hundred dollar bill.
  – *K-Lens-M Komments* (March, 1964)

❖ He who makes himself an ass must not take offense if men ride him.

❖ You can always figure out whether or not a fellow is crooked by viewing him from the right angle.

❖ There is no smaller package than a man wholly wrapped up in himself.

❖ If our faults were written on our faces, how many of us would hold our heads up?

❖ When singing your own praises don't get the key too high.
  – *K-Lens-M Komments* (September, 1963)

❖ Folks wouldn't worry so much about what others thought of them if they'd realize how seldom they did.

❖ It is just as difficult for some people to keep a promise as it is for others to save money.

❖ When a man is touchy about his dignity, it is a pretty good sign that he hasn't any.

❖ An optimist hopes for the best and makes the most of what he gets.

❖ One of the hardest secrets for a man to keep is his opinion of himself.

❖ The more faults you find, the more you have. – *K-Lens-M Komments* (September, 1963)

❖ A pat on the back develops character—if administered young enough, often enough, and low enough.

❖ No man believes others to be on the square after he has lost faith in himself.

❖ A coat of whitewash covers a multitude of spotted reputations.

❖ Our conscience is the loser when we try to argue with it.

❖ It's fine to believe in ourselves, but we mustn't be too easily convinced. – *Burton Hillis in Better Homes & Gardens*

❖ Using good deeds to cover up crookedness fools nobody but yourself.

❖ There are people who distrust those who flatter them and dislike those who don't. – *K-Lens-M Komments* (March, 1964)

❖ The fellow who bids for praise always buys the cheapest kind.

❖ How a person plays a game shows some of his character. How he loses shows all of it.

❖ Reputation is a bubble that a man blows; whether it bursts or not is up to him.

❖ Sometimes the fellow with an elastic imagination tries to use it for a conscience.

❖ He can be a man of his word and still be of little value.

❖ Reputation is what men and women think of us; character is what God and the angels know of us. – *Thomas Paine*

❖ One sure test of willpower is to see a friend with a black eye and not ask any questions.

❖ Take a very careful look at the fellow who insists on telling you how honest he is.

❖ It is humanly impossible to build a reputation on the things you are going to do.

❖ The wages of sin have no deductions. – *K–Lens–M Komments* (September, 1963)

❖ Envy shoots at others and wounds herself.

❖ A cynic is a man who has sized himself up and then got sore about it.

❖ Flattery is the art of telling the other fellow exactly what he thinks of himself.

❖ Beware of a two-faced individual. His specialty is manufacturing barefaced lies.

❖ How easy it is to remind the other fellow of the character building qualities of adversity.

❖ Very little talent is required to make a fool of yourself.

❖ He who mistrusts most should be trusted least.

❖ Adversity doesn't build character; it merely places what you have on exhibition.

❖ Even the man on the level has an uphill fight just to stay there.

❖ The same people who can deny others everything are famous for refusing themselves nothing.

❖ One's good breeding is the best security against another's bad manners.

❖ Egotism enables the man in a rut to think he's in the groove.

❖ To find out what a man is, find out what he does when he has nothing to do.

❖ Nearly all men can stand adversity, but if you want to test a man's character, give him power. – *Abraham Lincoln*

❖ The tragedy of today is not the noisiness of the bad people, but the silence of the good people.

❖ The faults of others are like headlights on an automobile. They always seem more glaring than our own.

❖ Occasionally reputations are lost; but usually we throw them away.

❖ Our view of our own faults is likely to be astigmatic. – *K-Lens-M Komments* (October, 1963)

❖ You can't get the true measure of a man when only one side of him is taken into account.

❖ Arrogance trips on its high heels; the humble seldom stumble.

❖ Another human weakness is the nice man's belief that wrong isn't wrong if done by a man like him.

❖ If we could see ourselves as others see us, the chances are we would deny it.

❖ A man's reputation sometimes casts a shadow over his character.

❖ Character is like a rifle; it cannot shoot higher than it is aimed.

❖ The fellow who goes right will have plenty of elbowroom.

❖ A defeat is sometimes a better character builder than an easy victory.

❖ Every man must live with the man he makes of himself.

❖ It takes a few hard knocks to reduce a swelled head.
  – *K-Lens-M Komments* (August, 1964)

❖ People who want to find fault can always find plenty of raw material wherever they are.

❖ We knew a fellow who was so conceited that he joined the navy so the world could see him.

❖ He who insists on talking about himself soon has a one-man audience.

❖ The daily grind helps give you an edge.

❖ An egotist thinks a mirror does a pretty good job.

❖ Look into the mirror occasionally; it will tell you exactly what the neighbors see.

❖ A resounding defeat is sometimes a better character builder than an easy victory.

❖ Know yourself—it is no misfortune to tumble to your faults.

❖ A good reputation may be merely proof that you do not have inquisitive neighbors.

❖ Those looking down on their inferiors have none.
   – *K-Lens-M Komments* (October, 1963)

❖ When a man speaks badly of you, so live that no one will believe him.

❖ Compliments should be treated like Christmas gift neckties— acknowledged and then put away and forgotten.

❖ One of the most likely uses of atomic energy seems to be the cooking of the world's goose. – *D. O. Flynn*

❖ Before you start exposing the faults of others count ten—ten of your own.

❖ Men who deserve monuments do not need them. – *Gene Fowler*

❖ There may be some good in every man, but some of them keep it bottled up pretty tight.

❖ Broken promises are the trademark of a weak character.

❖ Charm: Making someone think both of you are grand.
   – *K-Lens-M Komments*

❖ When a man has a "pet peeve" it's remarkable how often he pets it. – *Sydney J. Harris*

❖ Eggs and promises are easily broken.

❖ Some men are character actors—when they show any character, they're acting.

❖ You've got to be a little different if you want to get noticed. After all, would anyone give the Tower of Pisa a second glance if it were standing straight? – *Monique Van Vooren*

❖ When your honesty and integrity break down, you can find no place to get spare parts.

❖ Flattery isn't worth the fuss, unless it's being heaped on us. – *K-Lens-M Komments* (October, 1963)

❖ Breeding: the quality that enables a person to wait in well-mannered silence while the loudmouth gets the service.

❖ Many people never learn that uncovering the other fellow's faults will never cover up their own.

❖ Rudeness is a weak man's imitation of strength. — *Newsweek*

❖ The man without character has to depend on reputation to carry him through life's battles.

❖ Being two-faced will not double your face value.

❖ If a man has good or bad points, adversity will bring out his true colors.

❖ True character is measured by living the kind of life your admirers think you do.

❖ It is better to be silent and be thought a fool than to open your mouth and remove all doubt.

❖ People who fish for compliments usually have a big line.

❖ Most any fellow can prove that he has good sense. All he has to do is to say that you have.

❖ Reputation is like glass—easy to crack but hard to mend.

❖ Self-praise has no real value. Put it in the same class as anything else you get for nothing.

❖ Nothing removes conceit like a walk through the cemetery.

❖ Egotism is useful as an anesthetic for a person's stupidity.

❖ People who fish for compliments wait with baited breath.

❖ An inflated ego doesn't make you a swell guy. – *K-Lens-M Komments* (April, 1964)

❖ There's not much hope for the fellow who blackens his friends in an attempt to whitewash himself.

❖ Egotism is a drug that enables more people to live with themselves.

❖ Self-confidence is good, but always try to be in a position to back it up.

❖ The only time you should blow your own horn is when you're in the band.

❖ Nothing is as easy to make as a promise this winter to do something next summer; this is how commencement speakers are caught.

❖ Rare is the person who can weigh the faults of others without putting his thumb on the scales.

❖ People who keep up with their consciences set a good pace.

❖ Egotist: a person who is always letting off esteem.
 – *Paul F. Gilbert*

❖ Charm is a glow within a woman, which casts a most becoming light on others. – *John Mason Brown*

❖ Why all this talk of a poor loser—did you ever hear of a rich one?

❖ A man with a heart of gold seldom has much of it in the bank.

❖ Don't worry about what others think of you; they seldom do.

❖ It is sheer folly to judge a man by the opinion he has of himself.

❖ You can't be caught in a place of ill repute if you never go there.

❖ If a man intends to stand on his dignity, he should have spikes in his heels.

❖ You have become a mature person when keeping a secret gives you more satisfaction than passing it along. – *John M. Henry*

❖ An evil deed cannot bring honor.

❖ If you are all wrapped up in yourself, you're overdressed.

❖ Your word will be accepted by others only after you have proved you will keep it.

❖ Full-length mirrors were invented to keep us humble. – *K-Lens-M*

Komments (July, 1964)

❖ The genuine self-made man never considers himself finished.

❖ The average man is an excellent judge of human nature—except in his own case.

❖ The only way a man can become well heeled is to keep on his toes.

❖ Strive always to be like a good watch – open face, busy hands, pure gold, well regulated, and full of good works.

❖ Never wish to be anything but what you are, and try to be that perfectly.

❖ Habits form rails over which a man's train of thought must travel.

❖ The fellow who is thoroughly satisfied with himself is about as worthless as they come.

❖ He who stands for nothing will usually fall for anything.

❖ An egotist is a man who thinks that if he hadn't been born, people would have wanted to know why.

❖ A fault that humbles a man is of more use than a virtue that puffs him up.

❖ The one thing all charming people have in common, no matter how they may differ in other respects, is an amused detachment from their commonplace troubles. – *Sydney J. Harris, General Features Corp.*

❖ Never stand on your dignity. There's nothing more slippery.

❖ He not only starts things he can't finish, he starts things he can't even begin. – *Smiles*

❖ He who blows his own horn seldom succeeds. After all, it isn't the whistle that pulls the train.

❖ Many a person might have become outstanding but for fear of being different.

❖ Remember that you only have one chance to make a first impression.

❖ The ancient sage who concocted the maxim, "Know thyself," might have added, "Don't tell anyone." – *H. F. Henrichs*

❖ If we could see ourselves as others see us, we'd think there was something wrong with our eyes.

❖ A man can have no better epitaph than that which is inscribed in the hearts of his friends.

❖ Nothing is easier than faultfinding: no talent, no self-denial, no brains, and no character are required to set oneself up in the grumbling business.

❖ When you break your word, you break something that cannot be mended.

❖ Once you have mastered the rules of etiquette, you can ignore them.

❖ No etiquette book is needed to know what's in good form. – *K-Lens-M Komments* (August, 1965)

❖ They can do least who boast most.

❖ There is plenty of difference between a wise guy and a wise man.

❖ He who spends today in bragging about what he is going to do tomorrow, probably did the same thing yesterday.

❖ Meeting trouble halfway means poor company the rest of the way.

❖ Practice self-inspection; it prevents many cases of ego-itis.

❖ The man who would rather be right than popular usually winds up being neither.

❖ The speediest deflation is a punctured reputation.
– *K-Lens-M Komments* (August, 1963)

❖ He who places the blame for his downfall where it belongs is really a big man.

❖ Empty barrels make the most noise.

❖ Don't worry too much about what other people think of you. It is just about the same as what you think about them.

❖ I love criticism just so long as it's unqualified praise.
– *Noel Coward*

❖ Conscience is a still small voice that makes you feel still smaller.

Children

❖ Children sometimes tear it up, but they never break up a home.

❖ A picture window will bring the outdoors into a living room, but a little boy's feet will bring in more of it.

❖ A teacher asked a small boy to name five things that contain milk. He replied, "Butter, cheese, ice cream, and two cows."

❖ Children don't want to be told; they want to be shown. It takes years of telling to undo one unwise showing. – *Eileen M. Haase*

❖ One of the advantages of youth is that they haven't already seen the movies shown on TV.

❖ Judging by their noise, I've found, most children basically are sound. – *Margaret M. Ellert*

❖ A mother's life is not a happy one. She is torn between the fear that some designing female will carry off her son and that no designing male will do the same with her daughter.

❖ Many an unwanted child becomes wanted in all of our fifty states. – *K-Lens-M Komments* (October, 1965)

❖ The little girl who used to make faces at the boys now makes eyes at them.

❖ A teenager is grown up when he thinks it is more important to pass an examination than to pass the car ahead.

Children

❖ Autumn is when an unwatched boy, raking, leaves.
  – *The Wall Street Journal*

❖ Teach your child to hold his tongue; he'll learn fast enough to speak.

❖ What it now costs to amuse a child is more than it took to educate his parents.

❖ The advantage of a large family is that one of them at least may not turn out like the others.

❖ A man may wear a greasy hat and his trousers may be shiny, but if his children have their noses flattened against the windowpane a half hour before he is due home for supper, you can trust him with anything you have.

❖ A dog teaches a boy fidelity, perseverance, and to turn around three times before lying down. – *Robert Benchley*

❖ Train up a child in the way he should go—and the first thing you know he's gone.

❖ Nursery school: where small children go to catch colds from each other so they can stay home. – *Dorothy Truitt Reed*

❖ Triplets: do-it-yourself population explosion. – *K-Lens-M Komments*

❖ Adolescence is a time of rapid changes. Between the ages of 12 and 17, for example, a parent ages as much as 20 years.
  – *Changing Times, The Kiplinger Magazine*

❖ A perfect example of minority rule is a baby in the house.

❖ Out of the mouths of babes come things that grown-ups shouldn't have said in the first place.

❖ Heredity: something you believe in when your child's report card is all A's. – *E. E. Kenyon*

❖ Show us a home with young children and we'll show you a home where every pack of cards counts out at between 37 and 51.

❖ Children: unreasonable facsimiles. – *Jack Herbert*

❖ The hardest people to convince that they've reached retirement time are children. – *Arnold H. Glasgow*

❖ You've got to make allowances for children. After all, they make deductions for you.

❖ One of the first things one notices in a backward country is that children are still obeying their parents.

❖ A brat is a child who acts like your own, but belongs to a neighbor.

❖ Children, like canoes, are more easily controlled if paddled from the rear. – *Bill Stewart*

❖ The hardest job in the world is teaching children to keep from hurting the feelings of others without turning them into liars.

❖ Maternity ward: the only place in the world where there isn't a chance of evading the issue. – *Superior Cirkuts*

❖ Infant prodigy: small child with highly imaginative parents.

❖ A kindergarten teacher is one who knows how to make the little things count.

❖ One way to curb delinquency would be to take parents off the street at night.

❖ Adolescence is the time in a boy's life when he notices that a girl notices that he's noticing her.

❖ It's all right to tell a little boy not to cry because crying won't help—but that's not really honest advice to give a little girl.
– *Kingsport, Tennessee, Times*

❖ It is easier for a father to have children than for children to have a real father. – *Pope John XXIII*

❖ Child guidance is what more and more parents are getting from their children. – *Anthony J. Pettito*

❖ With three daughters, our problem hasn't been keeping the wolf from the door, but feeding the pack. – *Marcelene Cox*

❖ Parents spend the first part of a child's life getting him to walk and talk, and the rest of his childhood getting him to sit down and shut up. – *Mrs. Robert C. Tanner*

❖ The best time to put children to bed is when you can.

❖ Father to daughter's beau: "I'm glad to meet you, Johnny, but I somehow pictured you with a telephone attached to your head."
– *Marilyn Estep*

❖ A jail sentence is frequently a belated substitute for spanking.

❖ Four-year-old's definition of nursery school: a place where they try to teach children who hit, not to hit and children who don't hit, to hit back. – *Mrs. M. S. N.*

❖ Give a pig and a boy everything they want. You'll get a good pig and a bad boy.

❖ Most American children get the best of everything, including their parents.

❖ Things generally balance out. Other people's troubles are never as bad as our own, but their children are always a whole lot worse.

❖ Adolescence is that period in a child's life when his parents become more difficult.

❖ Children are often spoiled because you can't spank their grandparents.

❖ The way to keep teenagers out of hot water is to put dishes in it.

❖ There's nothing wrong with parents that their teenage daughter can't exaggerate. – *Lavonne Mathison*

❖ A switch has put many a delinquent on the right track.

❖ Son or daughter: your second chance. – *K-Lens-M Komments*

❖ Father: the parent who gets his daughter off his hands and then has to get his son-in-law on his feet.

❖ There was less juvenile delinquency when Dad used the woodshed as an administration building.

❖ Children and dogs are about the only things in a home that have to be washed by hand.

Children

❖ Some children are like canoes; to make them go straight, they must be paddled.

❖ They tell us that a baby first laughs at the age of four months. By then he can focus his eyes well enough to see what his daddy looks like.

❖ The fellow who remembers what he was taught at his mother's knee was probably bent over it. – *Minnesota Journal of Education*

❖ Some people never get over the spanking stage. After their parents stop, experience begins.

❖ If the world seems to beat a path to your door, you've probably got a teenage daughter.

❖ Did you ever wonder where mothers learn all the things they tell their daughters not to do?

❖ It is unfortunate that Providence didn't think to give us our neighbors' children, since these are the only ones we know how to raise. – *Don Rose*

❖ The actions of some children suggest that their parents embarked on the sea of matrimony without a paddle. – *W. Rogers in Swainsboro, Georgia, Forest-Blade, quoted in Atlanta Journal*

❖ Be very careful what you say in front of a parrot or a small child.

❖ Addle-essence: your children are growing up when your daughter starts putting on lipstick and your son starts wiping it off. – *Changing Times, The Kiplinger Magazine*

❖ Weary voice: "My life as a mother of three has been cerealized." – *Mildred Nelson Kain*

❖ Juvenile delinquency is the result of parents trying to train children without starting at the bottom.

❖ School-bus driver: a man who thought he liked children. – *Harold Coffin*

❖ Teenagers: people who get hungry again before the dishes are even washed. – *Dorothy B. Challman*

❖ If there's anything kids get a bang out of, it's a screen door. – *K-Lens-M Komments* (July, 1964)

❖ There is nothing so comforting as the patter of little children's feet about a home, because the moment the sound stops, one knows they are up to something they shouldn't be. – *Anonymous*

❖ Parents Can't Win Department: if a child isn't able to blame his mistakes on an improper bringing up, he'll manage to blame them on one that was too proper.

❖ You can convince a man and persuade a woman, but you have to ignore a teenager.

❖ Parent of a boy in college, "Our son is a four-letter man—we hear from him fall, winter, spring, and summer."

❖ Father walked three miles to school and enjoyed it. Son now walks six blocks and grumbles.

❖ Parents find it hard to believe all the things they expect their children to believe.

❖ Educators say that the character of a child is determined between the ages of two and five. It certainly is. – *Frances Rodman*

❖ After you have children, the economic law reverses to Demand

and Supply. – *Marcelene Cox*

❖ The needs of a student at college are known; pay him a visit and leave him a loan. – *Harold L. Taylor*

❖ You can tell that a child is growing up when he stops asking where he came from and starts refusing to tell where he's going. – *Changing Times, The Kiplinger Magazine*

❖ Some girls get tanned where it shows, but not where it's needed.

❖ My children are at the perfect age—too old to cry at night and too young to borrow my car. – *Walter Slezak*

❖ Many teenagers come home late at night to find a parent burning in the window instead of a light. – *Dan Bennett*

❖ Adolescence is when daughter knows best. – *William Franklin Gaines*

❖ About the only two things a child will share willingly are communicable diseases and his mother's age. – *The Wall Street Journal*

❖ One-year-old beginning to walk, talk, balk. – *Florence Gennes*

❖ Children cannot be made good by making them happy, but they can be made happy by making them good. – *E. J. Kiefer*

❖ April showers bring May flowers and kids cooped up in the house for hours. – *Changing Times, The Kiplinger Magazine*

❖ There are fewer problem children than children with problems. – *K-Lens-M Komments* (September, 1963)

❖ One stork said to another, "There's a mean streak in you, brother, or you wouldn't leave three babies at the house where the washing machine is broken down."

❖ Chaperone: one who is too old to get into the game, but still tries to intercept the passes. – *Tennessee Ernie Ford*

❖ A lot of us remember when a wayward child was straightened up by being bent over a chair.

❖ After a male has grown out of long dresses and triangles and has acquired pants, freckles, and so much dirt that relatives dare not kiss him between meals, it becomes a boy.

❖ Parents speak of the modern generation as if they had nothing to do with it. – *Tony Pettit*

❖ I am sure that if people had to choose between living where the noise of children never stopped and where it was never heard, all the good natured and sound people would prefer the incessant noise to the incessant silence. – *George Bernard Shaw*

❖ All that keeps some families from having a home of their own is a teenage daughter.

❖ Few children fear water unless soap is added.
   – *William Franklin Gaines*

❖ Modern psychology tells us that it's bad to be an orphan, terrible to be an only child, damaging to be the youngest, crushing to be in the middle, and taxing to be the oldest. There seems no way out, except to be born an adult. – *Woodmen of the World Magazine*

❖ A teenager sent his girl her first orchid with this note: "With all my love and most of my allowance."

❖ Teenager in coffeehouse: "I got my folks' permission to grow a beard, but nothing comes!" – *Cissie cartoon*

❖ Fathers are pals nowadays mainly because they haven't got guts enough to be fathers. – *Sam Levenson*

❖ Times do change. It is alarming the different methods modern day children use in bringing up their parents.

❖ Some parents will spend anything on their children except time. – *Maurice Seitter*

❖ The world started going to smash about the time it abandoned the hand-cranked ice-cream freezer, the finest device ever invented for teaching youth that work has its rewards. – *Cleveland News*

❖ Mealtime: when youngsters sit down to continue eating. – *The Office Economist*

❖ By the time we decide a television program is something the children shouldn't see, we're too interested in it ourselves to shut it off. – *Caper's Weekly*

❖ Child's allowance: a down payment on what he spends. – *Franklin P. Jones*

❖ Mothers who are a little sad as they send their small boys off to camp can look at it this way: they're not losing a son—they're gaining two turtles, a frog and a garter snake. – *Pat Buttram*

❖ As pretty as children on their birthdays. – *Truman Capote*

❖ A wise parent lets a child who throws a tantrum catch it. – *Margaret Yablonski*

❖ The handwriting on the wall usually means there's a child in the

family. – *Franklin P. Jones*

Surprising Facts by K-Lens-M Komments

- ✓ World population increases 120,000 daily—more than one each second. (June, 1962)
- ✓ The average mother puts in a 98-hour workweek. (May, 1963)
- ✓ U. S. population increases about 8,000 every hour. (May, 1963)

Communication & Conversation

❖ Where thought is shallow, vile language and a loud voice take the place of sound facts.

❖ Keep unkind words in your mouth; you may have to eat them later.

❖ The greatest trouble with small talk is that it comes in large doses.

❖ It is true that silence cannot be misquoted, but it can be misinterpreted.

❖ Talking comes by nature; silence by understanding.

❖ Repartee is something you think of after you have become a departee.

❖ Repartee is what you think you might have said after you get home and go to bed.

❖ We cannot always oblige, but we can always speak obligingly.
  – *Voltaire*

❖ Saying nothing at the wrong time can be just as effective as saying the right thing at the right time.

❖ Suppose everyone did think twice before they spoke; it would have a mighty depressing effect on conversation.

❖ The bone of contention is always the jaw.

❖ A modest person is one who does not blow his knows.

❖ Nature blunders, too. She often gives the biggest mouths to those who have the least to say.

❖ 'Tis a good word that can better a good silence.

❖ Wit is the salt of conversation, not the food. – *W. Hazlitt*

❖ The hardest thing for some people to say in 25 words or less is "Good-bye." – *Tony Pettito*

❖ Isn't it funny that what we overhear is far more interesting than what we should hear?

❖ Too much loose talk can get a person in a tight spot.

❖ It does little good to weigh your words if you are using crooked scales.

❖ Don't tell me what I mean—let me figure it out for myself. – *Frank Farrell*

❖ He's got an impediment in his speech. Every time he opens his mouth, his wife interrupts. – *Erskine Johnson*

❖ To say the least is not some people's way of doing it.

❖ Listening: silent flattery. – *K-Lens-M Komments*

❖ Let your speech be better than silence, or keep silent.

❖ The words that should be unsaid are too often the ones people like most to hear.

❖ The best argument is that which seems merely an explanation.
   – *Dale Carnegie*

❖ Jumping to conclusions doesn't always make for happy landings.
   – *Mail Order Trade*

❖ Nothing is more worthless than a reputation as a good speaker.

❖ Let a man talk about himself and he'll think you are interesting.

❖ Some speakers we have heard who said they had been given ten minutes, should have started at the ninth minute.

❖ After all is said and done, more is usually said.

❖ A gossip talks about others. A bore talks about himself. A brilliant conversationalist talks about you.

❖ Cooperate with nature. Our ears aren't made to shut—our mouth is. – *K-Lens-M Komments* (August, 1964)

❖ The best conversationalist may be the man who thinks twice and says nothing.

❖ She developed an impediment in her speech—she stops to think.
   – *Gene Sherman*

❖ There is nothing wrong with having nothing to say unless you insist on saying it.

❖ For a really fetching conversation, three persons are required: two to talk and one to be the topic.
   – *Dixie County Advocate, Cross City, Florida.*

❖ No man knows too much, but it is always easy to talk too much.

❖ If a thing will go without saying, let it.

❖ Blessed are they who have nothing to say, and cannot be persuaded to say it.

❖ Swear off talking so much and see what a good listener you become; besides, you might even learn something.

❖ Some speakers don't understand there is no connection between eloquence and endurance.

❖ The fellow who thinks he knows it all might get by with it if he knew just when to stop talking.

❖ In Balaam's time it was considered a miracle when an ass spoke; today it's a miracle when you can get one to shut up.

❖ Freedom of speech has enabled many a man to hang himself.

❖ Get into the habit of thinking pleasant thoughts. They may break into words any minute.

❖ It pays to use sweet talk—especially if you have to eat your words.

❖ Silence has never been known to make a blunder, and sometimes it makes a decided hit.

❖ A closed mouth gathers no feet. – *Bob Cooke*

❖ You can never hope to become a skilled conversationalist until you learn how to put your foot tactfully through the television set. – *M. Dale Baughman*

❖ Some people are not satisfied to tell all they know—they just keep on talking.

❖ She has a tongue that jaywalks over every conversation.
  – *Mary C. Dorsey*

❖ Many an after dinner speaker talks in his audience's sleep.

❖ Discussion is an exchange of intelligence. Argument is an exchange of ignorance. – *Washington Post and Times Herald*

❖ At least silence puts up a bluff that is mighty hard to call.

❖ I agree with you, but I must admit you're wrong.

❖ When engaged in a heavy conversation, be careful not to drop a remark.

❖ If you think twice before you speak, it will give the other fellow a chance to make a fool of himself.

❖ Printed letterheads are so useful. You can find out the name of the man who signed the letter.

❖ Tact is the ability to close your mouth before someone wants you to.

❖ Yesterday's gossipy back fence chat has been transferred to the laundromat. – *K-Lens-M Komments*

❖ To write well and speak well, one must have something to say.

❖ You can't prove yourself a good talker by doing all of it; comparisons are needed.

❖ Always feel sorry for the speaker who talks hesitatingly. He doesn't know just what he is going to say next, either.

❖ A slip of the foot you may soon recover, but a slip of the tongue you may never get over. – *Benjamin Franklin*

❖ Learn to hold your tongue; you can then hold your own in any company.

❖ It is with a word as with an arrow—once let loose it does not return.

❖ They always talk who never think.

❖ Words may become mental palaces that will live forever, or they may become shacks that the first breeze will carry away.

❖ If one can't back up what he says, he should have backed up before saying it.

❖ Secrets are like measles; they take easy and spread easy.

❖ Most of us have often regretted our speech, but seldom our silence.

❖ Every argument has two sides, but many of them have no end.

❖ Be not disturbed at being misunderstood; be disturbed at not understanding.

❖ When a fellow says, "Well, to make a long story short," it's too late. – *Don Herold*

❖ Many a choice whine is the product of sour grapes.
   – *Russell Newbold*

❖ Many an argument has been won by a negative reply given in a positive manner.

❖ There is no diplomacy like silence.

❖ Needed: a pocket scale for weighing our words.
   – *K-Lens-M Komments* (May, 1963)

❖ The teaching of public speaking in our schools doesn't go far enough; it teaches how to speak, but not when.

❖ If you can't get them to listen any other way, tell them it's confidential.

❖ What that loudmouth needs is a yapendectomy.
   – *Edward F. Murphy*

❖ It is dullest just before the yawn. – *K-Lens-M Komments* (July, 1964)

❖ There are times when silence is the best way to yell at the top of your voice.

❖ If a fellow can't improve the silence, he really ought not break it by stomping off.

❖ Those who multiply their words seldom add to their popularity.

❖ Tact: what a fellow has when he won't change his mind, but he can change the subject. – *Eddie Cantor*

❖ A Chinese philosopher tells us, "The swiftest horse cannot overtake the word one has spoken."

❖ The trouble with thinking twice before you speak is that you never get into the conversation. – *Arthur Murray*

❖ The difference between gossip and news depends on whether you hear it or tell it.

Timeless Teachings from Mrs. Stroupe's Blackboard

❖ A rumor is about as hard to unspread as butter.

❖ Pride loses its flavor when a man has to swallow his words.

❖ It's the smooth talking man that makes it rough for others.

❖ The human jaw is shrinking in size, but not from lack of exercise. – *K-Lens-M Komments*

❖ If silence is golden, we know a lot of people who have talked themselves out of huge fortunes.

❖ The sarcastic thing you left unsaid will never haunt you.

❖ Many wise words are spoken in jest, but they are far outnumbered by the foolish ones spoken in earnest.

Courage

- ❖ It is easy to be brave from a safe distance. – *Aesop*

- ❖ When trouble comes, wise men take to their work; weak ones take to the woods.

- ❖ You can't answer for courage if you have never been in danger.

- ❖ The best reason for holding your chin up when in trouble is that it keeps the mouth closed. – *Ivern Boyett*

- ❖ In the presence of trouble, some people grow wings; others buy crutches. – *Harold W. Ruopp*

- ❖ The test of courage is to know defeat without losing heart.

- ❖ One man with courage makes a majority.

- ❖ Keep up your courage and your courage will keep you up.

- ❖ Fear is a prison without bars.

- ❖ The difference between caution and cowardice: caution is when you are afraid, and cowardice is when the other fellow is afraid.

- ❖ To him who is in fear, everything rustles. – *Sophocles*

- ❖ Better face a danger once than be always in fear.

Drinking & Vices

❖ Alcohol very often puts the wreck in recreation.

❖ Some men can't make both ends meet because they are too busy making one end drink.

❖ Should a census be taken of all the Americans who are in the habit of drinking, we believe the results would be staggering.

❖ Bad habits cost money, but some folks seem to think they are worth the price.

❖ The good-intentioned man who is always going to turn over a new leaf has been known to lose his place entirely.

❖ One swallow doesn't make a summer, but it sure breaks a New Year's resolution. – *Will Rogers, Jr.*

❖ In prohibition days, many ships that passed in the night carried their own moonshine.

❖ Liquor: liquid abandon. – *K-Lens-M Komments* (October, 1965)

❖ Smoking makes women's voices harsh. If you want to prove it, try flicking ashes on the living room rug.

❖ Champagne is a drink that makes you see double and feel single.

❖ Social drinking is a lot like spelling Mississippi—it's mostly a matter of knowing when to stop. – *D. O. Flynn*

❖ Alcohol removes the finish from people faster than from furniture.

❖ When your eyesight begins to blur, you should use stronger glasses and weaker drinks.

❖ Have you tried the U.S. embassy cocktail? Two drinks and you're stoned! – *The GOP Newsletter*

❖ In me you see a happy man. Contentment fills my cup. I couldn't give up smoking, so I gave up giving up. – *Bob Goddard*

❖ Bartender: irrigation engineer. – *K-Lens-M Komments* (October, 1965)

❖ Sign in a bar: "Drink slowly—this bar checked by radar." – *Hal Fimberg*

❖ Some people have read so much about the harmful effects of smoking that they have decided to give up reading.

❖ Most of us can easily stop smoking—we've done it so many times.

❖ A pack a day could bring the mortician your way—you could end up in a flip-top box. – *K-Lens-M Komments* (March, 1964)

❖ You may have the right of way, but it isn't worth dying for.

❖ Tobacco is a plant consumed by two creatures—a large green worm and a man. The worm doesn't know any better.

❖ If you are rich and drink, you are an alcoholic; but if you are poor and drink, you are just a plain drunk.

❖ Then there was the ghost who walked into a pub and asked, "Do you serve spirits?"

❖ Are you smoking less and fuming more? – *K-Lens-M Komments* (March, 1964)

❖ You can be sure that drinking to a man's health isn't going to improve your own.

❖ When a man drinks to forget, the only thing he forgets is when to stop.

❖ One reason I don't drink is that I want to know when I am having a good time. – *Lady Astor, quoted in Christian Herald*

❖ Alcohol makes a man feel like he is a big gun just because he is carrying a heavy load.

❖ Double martinis: sips that passion the night. – *Sonny Eliot*

❖ Wash your hair in beer and you'll have the happiest dandruff in town.

❖ A hangover occurs when the brew of the night meets the cold of the day.

❖ If they had the hangover first, it might help reduce their thirst. – *K-Lens-M Komments*

❖ Thinking drivers don't drink; drinking drivers don't think.

❖ A boy begins to smoke to show he is a man. After 20 or 30 years, he tries to stop with the same objective.

❖ If you can remember when two ashtrays were enough for a seven-room house, brother, you are really an old-timer.

❖ Believing we do something when we do nothing is the first illusion of tobacco. – *Ralph Waldo Emerson*

❖ The driver is safer when the roads are dry; the roads are safer when the driver is dry.

❖ The man with a bundle of bad habits has the heaviest load in the world to carry.

❖ The people with bad habits are those who complain most of bad luck.

❖ Some smokers swear off . . . and on! – *K-Lens-M Komments* (March, 1964)

❖ A vacationer, arriving at a small mountain village, asked one of the natives, "Do the people here drink a lot of whiskey?" "Well," the mountaineer replied, "the water was turned off a while back and nobody knew it 'till Sam Jones' house caught fire."

❖ Bartender: a good mixer. – *K-Lens-M Komments* (April, 1964)

❖ Someone tells us of the newest drink—the Boy Scout Cocktail. A couple of drinks and a little old lady has to help YOU across the street.

❖ Gracie Allen explained how she knew when she'd had too much to drink: "A little blurred tells me." – *Earl Wilson*

❖ More good intentions would be carried out if they didn't get mixed up with bad habits.

❖ There are too many lit-and-run drivers. – *K-Lens-M Komments* (August, 1964)

❖ Now that they have made cigarettes less irritating, why don't they start working on the commercials?

❖ Dignity is one thing that cannot be preserved in alcohol.
– *Graeme and Sarah Lorimer*

❖ In the race of life, a strong drink can cause a weak finish.

❖ It seems a shame, when so many things we'd like to do are sinful, that it should also be wrong to do nothing. – *Frank Clark*

❖ When grandma used to tell you how many quarts and pints she put away, you knew she meant jellies and jams.

❖ A gallon of gas and a pint of gin frequently end up in a mess of tin.

❖ Only a light bulb can go out every night and still be bright the next day.

❖ To make a cigarette lighter, take out the tobacco.

❖ A hangover has been described as the wrath of grapes.

❖ Said a small boy to his father, "How come a soda pop will spoil my dinner and a martini gives you an appetite?"

❖ Atop a cigarette counter: "Draw your own conclusion."
  – *S. S. Biddle*

❖ Remember, driving a car on New Year's Eve is like Russian Roulette: you never know which driver is loaded.

❖ The coating of a gentleman is sometimes so thin that it comes off with a little alcohol.

❖ It is possible to get gallons of trouble out of a pint bottle.

❖ It's bad enough when a man is driven to drink, but it's even worse when he drives himself home from it.

❖ The only time that liquor makes a man go straight is when the road curves.

❖ Help others bear their burdens, but don't come home loaded every night.

❖ The trouble with whisky is that you take a drink and it makes a new man of you—then the new man has to have a drink.
  – *S. E. Robinson*

❖ Glasses have an amazing effect on vision—especially after they have been filled several times. – *Railway Carmen's Journal*

Surprising Facts by K-Lens-M Komments

✓ Alcoholic beverages have been used since the Stone Age. (May, 1965)

Driving

❖ Passing on hills and curves is a grave mistake.

❖ An automotive invention greatly needed is brakes that will automatically get tight when the driver does.

❖ One way of making ends meet is by driving too close to the car ahead.

❖ A motorist is a person who, after seeing a wreck, drives carefully for several blocks.

❖ Nothing improves your driving like having a police car following close behind you.

❖ A reckless driver is the one who passes you on the highway in spite of all your car can do.

❖ Passing the driver's test doesn't give you the right to pass everything on the road.

❖ You have less chance of reaching 70 if your car does. – *Albert Savage*

❖ Little drops of water, little flakes of snow, make the mighty traffic mighty slow. – *Philene Hammer*

❖ Men still die with their boots on—and one boot is frequently on the accelerator.

Driving

❖ When a man loses his self-control, it seems that his steering apparatus is broken.

❖ He who drives while drinking often gets a cop for a chaser.

❖ Notice to motorists: "Watch out for school children—especially if they are driving cars."

❖ Traffic is the mother-in-law of the otherwise perfect marriage between the American motorist and his car. – *Henry A. Barnes*

❖ Knowing the rules of driving safely is but half enough—you have to practice them.

❖ The rush hour is that time of day when traffic is practically at a standstill.

❖ It is better to sit tight than to attempt to drive when in that condition.

❖ He who pals around with vice soon becomes its slave.

❖ Remember, while driving on the highways, that other people can be as careless as you are.

❖ If these speed-crazed drivers knew they were driving to jail, they wouldn't be in such a hurry.

❖ It might be well for a motorist to remember that one foot on the brake is worth more than two in the grave.

❖ Courteous driving on the highways is a virtue some people expect others to have.

❖ Sign on a country road: "Drive carefully, there isn't a hospital within fifty miles."

❖ Bus sign: "Don't talk to driver. He needs both hands for driving."

❖ A judge's definition of an accident after hearing both drivers' stories: a head-on collision between two stationary cars parked on their own sides of the road.

❖ Sports car owner's daffynition of the typical American car: it's a four-eyed, one-horned, pink-and-purple Ethyl eater. – *Buck Herzog*

❖ One thing can be said about back seat drivers—they never lose control of the car.

❖ In looking for a good place to stop while out motoring, don't overlook the railroad crossings.

❖ You may get more than 40 winks if you fall asleep while driving. – *K-Lens-M Komments* (August, 1965)

❖ Red light: the place where you catch up with the motorist who passed you at 60 m.p.h. a mile back. – *Robert M. Lewis*

❖ Statistics show that locomotives are not afraid of automobiles.

❖ The way the traffic lanes are jammed, he who hesitates is rammed. – *Leonard K. Schiff*

❖ Said a woman driver to a friend who was riding with her, "Will you look how close that man is driving ahead of us?"

❖ Short cut: a route on which you can't find anybody to ask where you are. – *Franklin P. Jones*

❖ Motorists should drive as if they expected the pedestrians to do the unexpected.

❖ Puncture: a small hole in a tire, usually discovered a great distance from a garage.

❖ Mankind might take a lesson from the snowflake: no two are alike and yet look how beautifully they work together on major accomplishments, such as tying up traffic. – *Bill Vaughan*

❖ Only very few jaywalkers live long enough to qualify for old age pensions.

❖ America has a high rate of literacy but many can't read the traffic signs. – *K-Lens-M Komments* (October, 1963)

❖ The average man who looks under a car's hood doesn't know any more about it than the guy who used to look into a horse's mouth.

❖ Many a motorist whose eyes flit from limb to limb has hit a tree. – *Grand Island*

❖ Drive as if you are being trailed by a cop—and you won't be.

❖ Traffic Light: a trick to get pedestrians halfway across the street safely. – *Walter Winchell*

❖ The motorist who thinks money will buy everything never tried to buy spare parts for his body.

❖ My teenager says, in a tone of distress, that I don't understand his position. It seems that the key to his social success is the same one that fits the ignition.

❖ The best safety device is a careful driver. – *K-Lens-M Komments* (September, 1961)

❖ They say that fellows who fail their driver's license test become parking lot attendants.

❖ Some motorists drive like living was going out of style.
– *K-Lens-M Komments* (October, 1963)

❖ There is a safe way and a dangerous way to cross the street. The dangerous way is to try it on foot.

❖ The pedestrian has the right of way, especially in an ambulance.

❖ Fast drivers get everywhere a little sooner—even to the cemetery.

❖ Pedestrian: a person who should be seen and not hurt.
– *John Violette*

❖ Statistics show that the general run of pedestrians is a little too slow. – *Kathleen O'Dell in The Saturday Evening Post*

❖ A miss in the car is worth two in the engine.

❖ If you drive over seventy, be sure to keep an eye out for the other idiots.

❖ While driving along the highway, remember that you are under no obligation to transport a hitchhiker. He is just as useful where he is as anywhere else.

❖ The easiest way to lose control of your car is to forget to make the payments.

❖ Always heed highway signs. It's easier than taking advice from a nurse or undertaker.

❖ Pedestrian: person who can't find the place where he parked his car. – *Daily Mail, London.*

❖ The year 1963 proved that thousands died of gas. Some inhaled it, a few more lit it, and the rest stepped on it.

❖ Spare tire: the one you check the day after you have a flat.
– *Ken Kraft*

❖ Don't drive your car like an irresistible force—you may meet an immovable object.

❖ Traffic accidents are caused by these three classes of drivers: urban, suburban, and bourbon.

❖ Angels who guard you when you drive usually retire at 65.
– *Burma Shave Sign*

❖ There's a line on the ocean where you lose one day by crossing. There's one on the highways where you can do even better.

❖ The greatest hazards on highways are those under 21 driving over 65 and those over 65 driving under 21. – *Jim Reed*

❖ The driver who runs a traffic light is betting his life against a few seconds' time.

❖ Taximeter: a device for showing how fast you aren't getting there.
– *Marcelene Cox*

❖ You may have the right of way, but it's never worth dying for.

❖ Carefulness and carelessness on the highways are both habits. You can have your choice.

❖ The pioneers who blazed the trails now have descendants who burn up the roads. – *The Postage Stamp*

❖ America's motorists take good care of their cars—and they keep pedestrians in good running condition.

❖ A pedestrian may be in the wrong, but he still doesn't deserve the death penalty.

❖ You can't judge the power of an automobile by the exhaust, nor the man.

❖ Wonder if anybody has taken the time to enumerate how many things can go wrong with an automobile?

❖ For that rundown feeling, try jaywalking. – *K-Lens-M Komments*

❖ When you make a right turn from a left-hand lane, chances are you are just absent-mined, and not really what the driver behind called you.

❖ Pedestrian: a husband who didn't think the family needed two cars. – *Bruce Patterson*

❖ A good driver may not get the recognition he deserves, but neither will his family receive sympathy cards.

❖ Don't hit a man when he's down or a pedestrian when he's up. – *K-Lens-M Komments* (March, 1964)

❖ Any car will last a lifetime if you are a careless driver.

❖ It's not the used cars that are dangerous; it's the misused ones.

❖ Don't drive as if it were a matter of life or death—sometimes it happens to be just that.

❖ If more motorists were willing to give ground, there would be fewer of them in it.

Driving

❖ If all the cars in the world were placed end-to-end, some dope would pull out and try to pass them.

❖ Nowadays a pedestrian is one who walks from the house to the garage.

❖ Wait for traffic lights to change. It takes less time than to get patched up in a hospital.

❖ Traffic will soon be so heavy that we'll have to travel the main highways by appointment only.

❖ Drive so that your driver's license will expire before you do.

❖ Frequently the last word in an automobile is "step on it."

❖ Traffic warning sign in a small town: "Go slow. This is a one-hearse town."

❖ There are two well-known finishes for automobiles—lacquer and liquor.

❖ Pedestrian: a man who thought there were still a couple gallons of gas left in the tank. – *The Wall Street Journal*

❖ A ferryboat is something that makes every passenger cross.

Surprising Facts by K-Lens-M Komments

✓ The average auto salesman makes about 25 actual sales pitches to sell one car. (June, 1962)
✓ U.S. motorists get 70,000,000 traffic tickets yearly. (May, 1963)
✓ In 1900, all the hard-surfaced roads in the U. S. would not have linked New York and Boston. (August, 1963)

Timeless Teachings from Mrs. Stroupe's Blackboard

✓ City drivers make about 50 decisions per hour. (October, 1963)
✓ In most fatal pedestrian accidents, the pedestrian is at fault. (July, 1964)

Education & Learning

❖ Education: what's left over after you've forgotten the facts.
   – *Memphis Transit News*

❖ Education: the ability to quote Shakespeare without crediting it to the Bible. – *Evan Esar*

❖ Education benefits a man very little if he can't recognize an opportunity when he sees it.

❖ A father who wants his children to get an education these days may have to pull a few wires—the television wire, the hi-fi wire and the radio wire. – *Lavonne Mathison*

❖ The professor who comes in 15 minutes late is rare—in fact, he's in a class by himself. – *Virginia Tech Engineer*

❖ Education does not mean teaching people to know what they do not know; it means teaching them to behave as they do not behave. – *John Ruskin*

❖ For every schoolboy with a spark of genius, there are a dozen with ignition trouble. – *Shannon Fife*

❖ Education that fails to inform the mind and teach it to reason things out is useless.

❖ A schoolteacher philosophizes at 3 p.m.: "I'm too young to be as old as I am!" – *John J. Monzillo*

❖ The best of schools is the family fireside. – *K-Lens-M Komments*
   (October, 1963)

❖ The aim of education is not to impart as many isolated facts as
   possible. Nor is it merely to fit the pupil for a gainful occupation.
   The purpose of education should be to qualify the young for
   leading the best, the fullest and most useful life possible.
   – *R. B. Kuiper*

❖ Education may broaden a narrow mind, but there is no cure
   for conceit.

❖ A little learning is *not* a dangerous thing to one who does not
   mistake it for a great deal. – *William Allen White*

❖ Quantity production of college graduates doesn't cheapen the
   cost. – *K-Lens-M Komments*

❖ A good teacher is one who, when she calls upon herself, finds
   somebody home.

❖ The test of a truly educated man is what he is, what he thinks,
   and what his mind absorbs, dreams, or creates, when he is alone.
   – *Donald K. David, former Dean of Harvard's Graduate School of
   Business Administration*

❖ College: an institution that sometimes lowers entrance
   requirements with an end in view—not to mention
   promising tackles and backs. – *General Features Corp.*

❖ The only thing kids wear out faster than shoes are teachers.
   – *K-Lens-M Komments* (September, 1963)

❖ A local teacher received the following note: "My Claude is so
   sensitive. Don't ever punish him. Just slap the boy next to Claude;
   that will frighten him."

❖ It is never too late to learn; unlearning is quite another matter. – *K-Lens-M Komments* (May, 1965)

❖ One teacher reports that her pupils are full of the new math, the new English, the new geography and the same old excuses. – *Bill Vaughan*

❖ Some people who have very little formal education can make up for it with lots of understanding.

❖ One pound of learning requires ten pounds of common sense to apply it.

❖ Schooldays are the happiest of your life—providing, of course, your youngsters are old enough to go. – *California Grocers Advocate*

❖ Asked a local schoolteacher, "Johnny, why are you scratching yourself?" The lad replied, "Because no one else knows where I itch."

❖ Those who go to college and never get out are called professors.

❖ Education: the antidote for ignorance. – *K-Lens-M Komments* (August, 1963)

❖ On a dormitory door: "If I'm studying when you enter, wake me up."

❖ There was the man who spent $6,000 sending his son to college and all he got was a quarterback.

❖ Johnny says school would have more savor if he got time off for good behavior. – *K-Lens-M Komments*

❖ No one is too old to learn, but many people keep putting it off.

❖ The art of teaching is the art of assisting discovery.
  – *Mark Van Doren*

❖ June is busting out all over, and all a youngster wants out of
  school is himself. – *Toledo Blade*

❖ If you don't think every child in America is getting a higher
  education, brother, you haven't been paying taxes.

❖ It's never too late to learn—or too early. – *K-Lens-M Komments*
  (April, 1964)

❖ Everyone has to live and learn, but too many folks live faster than
  they learn.

❖ In the school of experience, you give out your own assignments
  and you don't skip classes.

❖ A man could learn many important things if he didn't think that
  he already knew them.

Entertaining

❖ No formal dinner is complete without nuts. Always invite a few.

❖ Nothing is more irritating than not being invited to a party you wouldn't be caught dead at. – *Bill Vaughan*

❖ The truly free man is the one who will turn down an invitation to dinner without giving an excuse. – *Jules Renard*

❖ The perfect host is the one who gives the party you are the life of. – *Alma Denny*

❖ The main ingredient in the recipe for successful after-dinner speaking is shortening.

❖ In every feast, remember that there are two guests to be entertained: the body and the soul; and that what you give to the body, you will presently lose, but what you give to the soul remains forever. – *Epictetus*

❖ Guests should not forget to go home.

❖ The man who is always the life of the party will be the death of his wife. – *Fred Sparks*

❖ The more circuitous route a story travels the better it seems to get.

❖ A party is a thing at which your wife gives her friends better food than you get all the week.

❖ Cocktail party: gathering at which drinks mix people.
 – *Guardian Chemical pamphlet*

❖ Keep your after-dinner speeches short. The capacity of the mind to absorb is limited to what the seat can endure.

❖ Bore: a person who sees that your company leaves at a reasonable hour. – *Tony Pettito*

❖ After-dinner speaking is the art of saying nothing briefly.

Faith

- ❖ The everyday Christian has a seven-to-one chance over the Sunday practitioner.

- ❖ Don't expect your wife to get you into heaven just because she was able to keep you out of jail.

- ❖ Who rises from prayer a better man, his prayer is answered.

- ❖ When a cannibal eats a missionary, it could be said that he got his first taste of religion.

- ❖ Some preachers should remember that the eternal doesn't require an everlasting sermon.

- ❖ Religion is a cloak used by some people in this world who will be warm enough without one in the next week.

- ❖ Blessings come in disguise. Most of us get what we deserve without recognizing it.

- ❖ Biscuits and sermons are improved by shortening.

- ❖ Some people wouldn't recognize the religion they profess if they were to meet it face to face.

- ❖ Set a good example and you preach a sermon without words.

- ❖ God often visits us, but most of the time we are not at home.

❖ Don't pin your faith to first guesses until you have given your decision a second thought.

❖ The church too many people belong to is the "Seventh Day Absentists." – *H. G. Hutcheson*

❖ We cannot get nearer heaven by standing on a brother's neck.

❖ Religion is the best armor in the world, but the worst cloak. – *Anonymous*

❖ One reason why it's difficult to get men to church is that they don't care what other men are wearing.

❖ No man ever loses religion—his religion loses him.

❖ The average American needs an adding machine to count his blessings. – *K-Lens-M Komments* (March, 1964)

❖ Don't lose faith because a few laws are being broken—look at the Ten Commandments.

❖ Religion often gets credit for reforming old rascals when old age is really responsible.

❖ Faith is an asset, but don't expect it to do the impossible.

❖ Don't preach unless you can practice if the occasion arises.

❖ Look at the trouble caused by a third party in the Garden of Eden. – *K-Lens-M Komments* (August, 1964)

❖ Most of us spend the first six days of each week sowing wild oats and then we go to church on Sunday and pray for a crop failure. – *Fred Allen*

❖ Glory paid to our ashes comes too late.

❖ You can often tell where one is going hereafter by what he goes after here.

❖ If all of us practiced religion, no one would have to talk religion.

❖ One of the fine things about silent prayer is that it shuts out the noise of the world. – *Dwight D. Eisenhower*

❖ It is strange that in praying we seldom ask for a change of character, but always for a change in circumstances.

❖ The man who puts aside his religion because he is going into society is like one taking off his shoes because he is about to walk on thorns.

❖ Too many people seem to prefer a religion that is not too hard on the conscience.

❖ There are two parts to the Bible: believing it and behaving it.

❖ Some folks never get enough religion to make them look pleasant, even in church.

❖ Faith is no problem to a man who has confidence in himself.

❖ Thrift is a good habit, but too many people try to economize on religion.

❖ Some people can talk more religion in a few minutes than they practice in a lifetime.

❖ Although religion is free, many people make a little of it go a long way.

❖ Religion and business that cannot mix have no business to meddle with anything.

❖ What we are is God's gift to us. What we become is our gift to God. – *Louis Nizer*

❖ Faith will ease people over the jolts and hard places on life's highway.

❖ Some people are mighty firm in their prejudices and weak in their faith.

❖ The brand of faith some people think will move a mountain wouldn't move a molehill.

❖ Eve: the first chicken to ruin a garden. – *K-Lens-M Komments* (May, 1965)

❖ Pray devoutly, but hammer stoutly.

❖ It is no use walking anywhere to preach unless we preach as we walk. – *St. Francis of Assisi*

❖ The worst moment for an atheist is when he feels grateful and has no one to thank. – *Samuel McCrea Cavert*

❖ Your religion is the life you live, not the creed you profess.

❖ Adam was first to overturn a new leaf.

❖ If all obeyed the Ten Commandments, there would be very little news.

❖ A religion that is small enough for our understanding would not be large enough for our needs. – *Arthur Balfour*

Faith

❖ The roots of evil seem to be planted very firmly.

❖ Don't think you are resting your faith because you fall asleep in church.

❖ Russia has abolished God, but so far God has been more tolerant. – *John Cameron Swayze*

❖ Faith is the bird that sings when the dawn is still dark.

❖ A local minister recently announced there are 786 sins. He is now being besieged by requests for the list by people who think they are missing something.

❖ Break faith with your fellow man, and you'll never break even.

❖ Many will argue that you cannot pray yourself out of trouble, but few will argue that you ever pray yourself into trouble.

❖ A minister preaches more by his square dealing than by his shouting.

❖ If you are not so close to God as you once were, you can be very certain as to which one of you moved.

❖ Some people never resort to prayer until they have tried everything else.

❖ The little boy who fired his cap pistol in church probably scared the devil out of more people than the preacher did.

❖ Wonder if Eve had cause for despair besting over which leaf to wear? – *K-Lens-M Komments* (July, 1964)

❖ A local teacher asked little Johnny if he would like to go to heaven. He replied, "Yes, but my mother told me to come right home after school."

❖ To be a good Christian, a man must back up his preacher all the week and then face him on Sunday.

❖ Prayers should be the key of the day and the lock of the night.

Family

❖ If your wife and children and dog think you are a great guy, why should you care what the rest of the world thinks?

❖ Having no family tree, many a man has succeeded because he branched out for himself.

❖ When Grandma was a girl she didn't do the things girls do today. But then grandmas didn't do the things grandmas do today. – *Joliet-Statesville, Time*

❖ Parents are people who bear infants, bore teenagers, and board newly-weds.

❖ It is indeed a desirable thing to be well descended, but the glory belongs to our ancestors. – *Plutarch*

❖ Retirement: when you exchange the currency in your billfold for snapshots of your grandchildren. – *K-Lens-M Komments* (September, 1963)

❖ Try to live up to the reputation your ancestors built—not on it.

❖ Small boy's definition of hotel: where you stay when you ain't got no cousins. – *Effie J. Bengston*

❖ The best way for a housewife to have a few minutes alone at the end of the day is to start doing the dishes. – *A. M. A. Journal*

❖ Telegram from a new father to his mother: "Congratulations. You have just become a babysitter." – *Clyde Ragsdale*

❖ One difference between outlaws and in-laws is that the latter usually promise to pay it back. – *Marietta, Ohio, Times*

❖ Avoid family quarrels in public. They allow a lot of truth to leak out.

❖ You have to give parents of big families a lot of credit; they can't get along without it.

❖ Blood is thicker than water—and it boils quicker.
– *Burnly Express and News*

❖ In most households, Mother is the softer voice, but Father is the softer touch. – *Hal Chadwick*

❖ The family tree is worth bragging about if it has consistently produced good timber, and not just nuts.

❖ A pretty good marriage counselor is the tot who tries to hug Mommy and Daddy at the same time. – *John M. Henry*

❖ The worst examples of snap judgment are usually found in a family photo album. – *Ken Kraft*

❖ It causes mixed emotions when you see your mother-in-law drive off a cliff in your new convertible.

❖ It is nothing short of miraculous how some family trees survive the underbrush.

❖ No man is good because his grandfather was. – *Ben Johnson*

❖ The Middle Years: that quiet, peaceful, serene period between completing the children's college education and starting in to help with the first grandchildren. The middle years usually last from three to five months. – *David Savage*

❖ Division in the family circle is a very unsatisfactory kind of arithmetic.

❖ Forget about your ancestors and concentrate on being an ancestor worth bragging about.

❖ The trouble that jet planes have got us into is that there are no longer any distant relatives. – *Farm Journal*

❖ Boys trying to follow in the footsteps of successful fathers should try to remember that their fathers didn't wear loafers.

❖ It's going to be hard for today's younger generation to think of something to tell their children they had to do without.

❖ Mothers are the highest paid—in love. – *K-Lens-M Komments* (May, 1964)

❖ When two prospective mothers-in-law meet, it's like a meeting between two horse traders; each one suspicious of what the other is unloading. – *Marcelene Cox*

❖ A mother-in-law is a referee with an interest in one of the fighters. – *E. E. Kenyon*

❖ Absence is one of the most useful ingredients of family life, and to dose it rightly is an art like any other. – *Freya Stark*

❖ Build a name for yourself. Don't live in the shadow of the name your ancestors built.

❖ Family tradition is a fine thing only when used to set a course in life—not as an anchor.

❖ It's a mistake for the woodman to spare some family trees.

❖ Without history, we wouldn't be able to use our ancestors' record as an alibi.

❖ To some people, home is just a filling station.

❖ Sometimes the poorest judge of distance is the family man who thinks he'll be able to make both ends meet. – *Earl Wilson*

❖ Genealogy: tracing yourself back to people better than you. – *John Pollard*

Surprising Facts by K-Lens-M Komments

✓ The average U.S. family of four uses 550 gallons of water daily. (September, 1963)

Food

❖ Laugh and the world laughs with you. Peel onions and you weep alone.

❖ There may be a destiny that shapes our ends, but our middles are of our own chewsing.

❖ We would have no objection to people who eat like sparrows if they would only stop that everlasting chirping about it.

❖ The hardest thing to raise in a garden is your aching back.
  – *K-Lens-M Komments* (June, 1962)

❖ An optimist gardener is one who believes that whatever goes down must come up. – *Floyd R. Miller*

❖ It is claimed that the average waiter walks about 14 miles a day. No wonder the soup is cold by the time you get it!
  – *K-Lens-M Komments*

❖ A small boy's idea of a balanced meal is a piece of cake in each hand. – *Jo Mark*

❖ A large percentage of accidents happen in the kitchen, and most of us have to eat them and pretend to enjoy them.

❖ Little snax—bigger slax. – *Ruth S. Schenley*

❖ Americans eat 36 billion sandwiches a year—the figures show.

❖ Advice to one on a diet: if at first you don't recede, try, try again.

❖ A watched pot certainly keeps a fellow on a diet. – *Vesta M. Kelly*

❖ Every man in the world reaps what he sows—except the amateur gardener. – *Cholly Knickerbocker, King Features*

❖ Picnic: living from sand to mouth. – *K-Lens-M Komments* (August, 1963)

❖ Nowadays apples are so expensive that you might as well have the doctor. – *Burton Hillis*

❖ Where there's smoke, there's a cookout! – *K-Lens-M Komments*

❖ Probably nothing in the world arouses more false hopes than one good cantaloupe. — *Pacific Northwest Cooperator*

❖ Doctors say that if you eat slowly you will eat less—and this is particularly true if you are a member of a large family. – *Lucia Hamilton*

❖ Picnic: when you bring along the mustard but forget the sandwiches. – *K-Lens-M Komments* (June, 1962)

❖ Coffee growers keep pushing for higher prices. Trouble may be brewing! – *K-Lens-M Komments* (April, 1964)

❖ Casserole: a method used by ingenious cooks to get rid of leftover leftovers. – *Barnes cartoon*

❖ All some folks do is eat, drink and complain. – *K-Lens-M Komments*

❖ Some people are no good at counting calories, and they have the figures to prove it.

Food

❖ Most men take a rather dim view of dining by candlelight.
   – *Arnold Glasgow* – *K-Lens-M Komments* (August, 1963)

❖ The hand is quicker than the eye is, but somewhat slower than
   the fly is. – *Richard Armour*

❖ Never bite the hand that feeds you—it may be your own.
   – *K-Lens-M Komments* (May, 1963)

❖ It takes a lot of will power to stop at eating one salted peanut.

❖ Calorie fighters spend too much time fraternizing with the
   enemy. – *K-Lens-M Komments* (October, 1963)

❖ On a milk truck: Don't be quart short. – *Amelia Kaufman*

❖ Square meals often make round people.

❖ Most families live from can to mouth.

❖ Diet: breadth control. – *K-Lens-M Komments* (October, 1963)

❖ Why not go out on a limb? Isn't that where the fruit is?
   – *Frank Scully*

❖ Rich food and late hours are what make a lot of people thick
   and tired.

❖ Diets are for those who are thick and tired of it. – *Paul Crume*

❖ A pessimist sees a stomach ache in every apple blossom.

❖ A picnic is when you take what you have in the house, put it
   between slices of bread, drive to some distant spot, and share it
   with the ants.

❖ Americans have more food to eat than any other people, and more diets to keep them from eating it.

❖ Most picnic lunches have everything from soup to gnats.
– *K-Lens-M Komments* (July, 1964)

❖ Just because a woman roasts her neighbors is no reason why she should be called a good cook.

❖ Burp: voice from within we can do without. – *K-Lens-M Komments* (March, 1964)

❖ Prune: plum, tuckered out. – *Bonnie Blaser*

❖ The dog is man's best friend, but the hot dog is the best dog—it feeds the hand that bites it.

❖ You don't have to eat grapefruit to get an eyeful. – *K-Lens-M Komments* (August, 1965)

❖ Part of the secret of success in life is to eat what you like and let the food fight it out inside. – *Mark Twain*

❖ Sign in a restaurant: Duncan Hines never ate here; he couldn't find a stool.

❖ TV dinners aren't so bad if they're not re-runs. – *K-Lens-M Komments*

❖ An apple a day keeps the doctor away. An onion a day keeps everybody away.

❖ The extent of a man's appetite for supper often depends on how many sandwiches his wife ate at the bridge party that afternoon.

❖ There's a tranquilizer cheese dip for folks who like quiet parties. – *K-Lens-M Komments*

❖ More people commit suicide with a fork than any other weapon.

Surprising Facts by K-Lens-M Komments

✓ Garlic reveals itself in perspiration as well as breath. (May, 1963)
✓ The milk produced in the world each year—put in quart bottles placed side by side—would circle the globe 400 times. (October, 1963)
✓ There are 81 kinds of edible eggs other than chicken eggs. (October, 1965)
✓ The average consumption of beer is higher in England than in Germany. (October, 1965)
✓ The most popular beverage in the world is tea. (October, 1965)
✓ Some wines are made without sugar. (October, 1965)
✓ It takes about 16 average oranges to make a quart of juice. (October, 1965)
✓ Tea shouldn't be steeped longer than three minutes. (October, 1965)
✓ Milk will boil quicker than water. (October, 1965)

Forgiveness

❖ When some people apologize, they are simply laying the foundation for a future offense.

❖ An apology, like a poultice, seldom draws the soreness out.

❖ It is good to forgive and forget, but some folks seem determined to see to it that you don't forget.

❖ A radio commentator stated the other day that women forgive more easily than men. Perhaps he is right because women get more practice.

❖ The right thing to do is to forgive and forget, but most people can't do two things at once.

Friendship

- It is easier to count your friends than it is to count on them.

- It is less trouble to make enemies than friends, but friends are worth the trouble.

- One of the most severe tests of friendship is to tell your friend of his faults.

- The friends you buy have to be paid a regular salary if you want to keep them.

- The man who hasn't got an enemy doesn't need one; all of his friends hate him.

- People who spend all their affections on themselves seldom collect dividends of friendship.

- Be friendly with the folks you know. Were it not for them, you would be a total stranger.

- Taking advantage of a raft of friends is the only thing that keeps some people afloat.

- There'll be no universal peace as long as one neighbor raises chickens while another tries to raise a garden. – *K-Lens-M Komments*

- He who insists on having his own way will find that his friends quickly get out of it.

❖ Inherit a lot of money and you won't have to pick your friends, they'll pick you.

❖ A true friend is one who doesn't consider it a permanent job when you have made a fool of yourself.

❖ It's not good to waste all your time loving your enemies; try treating your friends a little better.

❖ No man can climb very high by pulling his friends down.

❖ Lifelong friends get together once in a lifetime. – *K-Lens-M Komments* (April, 1964)

❖ A friend in need usually needs all you are willing to give and then some.

❖ It's nice to see people with a lot of get up and go, especially if they are visiting you.

❖ A few enemies will make a man more successful than a hundred friends.

❖ Friends: do-it-yourself relatives. – *K-Lens-M Komments* (September, 1963)

❖ When a man loses all his money, half of his friends don't know him anymore; the other half don't know he had lost it.

❖ About the most flattering thing we can say about our enemies is that we know where they stand. – *Douglas Meador*

❖ A friend overlooks your defects and, if he's fond of you, he doesn't see any. – *Arnold Glasgow*

❖ Friends who are full of devotion when we need no help are like pine trees that offer their shade in winter.

❖ Trouble is a sieve through which we sift our acquaintances. Those who are too big to pass through are our friends.

❖ The happiest miser of them all is he who keeps his friends.

❖ Many men pay so much attention to their enemies that they forget their friends.

❖ Lend a friend ten dollars, and you either lose a friend or ten dollars.

❖ Bonds of friendship grow stronger with age. – *K-Lens-M Komments* (October, 1963)

❖ It is sometimes necessary to make an enemy or two to clear up the atmosphere.

❖ It is far easier to count your friends than to count on them.

❖ No one has so big a house that he does not need a good neighbor.

❖ Hospitality is the art of making people feel at home when you wish they were.

❖ Constant use will wear out anything—especially friends.

❖ A cold shoulder will never attract warm friends.

❖ Some borrowing neighbors take everything but a hint.
 – *K-Lens-M Komments*

❖ Don't talk about yourself—your friends will when you leave.

❖ The wise thing to do is to divide all people into two classes—

friends and strangers. Friends we love too well to gossip about; strangers we know too little. – *Heywood Broun*

❖ Old friends, like old shoes, should not be discarded before the new ones are broken in.

❖ If you were someone else, would you want to be friends with you?

❖ I never thrust my nose into other men's porridge. It is no bread and butter of mine; every man for himself, and God for us all. – *Cervantes*

❖ Lend a hand to a friend in trouble and you can be sure he'll remember you—the next time he's in trouble.

❖ Love your enemies—it will drive them to distraction.

❖ No matter how many friends a man has, there comes a time when he has too few.

❖ If a man fails to make new friends as he passes through life, he will soon find himself alone.

❖ The finest kind of friendship is between people who expect a great deal of each other but never ask it. – *Sylvia Bremer*

❖ Real friendship comes when two people get so thick they can't see through each other.

❖ Humanity is fickle. Friends may toast you today and roast you tomorrow.

❖ In olden times a man with a grudge against his neighbor built a "spite" fence. Today he buys his son a saxophone.

Friendship

❖ A good neighbor is one who smiles at you over the back fence, but does not try to climb it.

❖ Many people use friendship as a drawing account and never think of making a deposit.

❖ Occasionally friends help a man find his place in the world—others put him in his place.

❖ The fire you kindle for your enemy often burns yourself worse than him.

❖ He is a friend to none who is a friend to all.

❖ Female friends: women mad at the same person. – *Electric Farmer*

❖ Friends don't expect explanations, and your enemies won't believe them.

❖ You may find the worst enemy or best friend in yourself.

Government & Politics

❖ Our forefathers founded an enduring nation. It is, however, enduring much more than they had planned for it.

❖ A foreign country is where people tell Americans to go home and leave them a loan.

❖ An old-timer is one who remembers when rockets were just a part of the fireworks display on the Fourth of July.

❖ We took this country from the Indians who scalped us, and then gave it to the politicians who skin us.

❖ Conservative: one who wants you to keep your hand out of his pocket. – *The Ave Maria*

❖ They don't hang men with wooden legs in China—they use rope.

❖ Our future as a nation is going to depend not so much on what happens in outer space as on what happens in inner space—the space between our ears.

❖ The price of liberty is vigilance—always payable in advance.

❖ A real diplomat is a man who has the ability to convince people they want what he wants them to have.

❖ All the Constitution guarantees is the pursuit of happiness. You have to catch up with it yourself. – *Benjamin Franklin*

❖ Freedom of speech is our greatest safety, because if a man is a fool the best thing to do is to encourage him to advertise the fact by speaking.

❖ George Washington was never licked until he got on a postage stamp, and he has his back turned then.

❖ An American is free to choose his own form of government—blonde, brunette or redhead. – *Columbia, S.C., State*

❖ Diplomat: one who can keep his shirt on while getting something off his chest. – *Calendar of Ninth Federal Savings and Loan Association*

❖ The country wouldn't be in such a mess today if the Indians had adopted more stringent immigration laws.

❖ America: Land of Hopportunity. – *K-Lens-M Komments* (May, 1965)

❖ What this country needs is someone who knows what this country needs.

❖ In America we can say what we think, and even if we can't think, we can say it anyway. – *Charles F. Kettering*

❖ "The right," be your battle cry ever, in waging the warfare of life, and God, who knows who are the heroes, will give you the strength for the strife. – *Phoebe Cary*

❖ It seems to us that heads, hearts and hands would settle the world's difficulties much more satisfactorily than arms.

❖ The greatest undeveloped resources of any nation are its people.

❖ What this country needs right now is someone who can foretell the future and then change it.

❖ America is a nation where a citizen will cross the ocean to fight for democracy [sic]—and won't cross the street to vote in a national election. – *Bill Vaughan*
  * The United States of America is a constitutional republic, not a democracy.

❖ Diplomacy: saying nothing nicely. – *K-Lens-M Komments*

❖ We've never had it so good or taken away from us so fast. – *Don Raihle*

❖ Nikita Khrushchev used to say that our children would live under Communism. Now he says that our grandchildren will live under Communism. So there's been some progress—we've saved a whole generation. – *David Brinkley*

❖ Determination has made our nation. – *K-Lens-M Komments*

❖ Great leaders and dedicated followers make a winning team.

❖ Remember that American still ends in "I can." – *Worcester, Massachusetts, Gazette*

❖ Diplomacy: the art of jumping into trouble without making a splash. – *Art Linkletter*

❖ "The home of the brave" is any home built at today's prices.

❖ A good citizen should always remember that one's country is bigger than one's party.

❖ The easiest way to get ahead of Russia is to get behind America.

❖ Give some people an inch and they think they are rulers.

❖ Government statistics collect facts and draw their own confusions.

❖ A statesman is a politician you agree with.

❖ Politics must be played by ear. – *K-Lens-M Komments* (October, 1965)

❖ It's hard for Uncle Sam to keep his balance with his hands in his pockets.

❖ Too many persons think the government should not only guarantee them a chance to pursue happiness, but should run interference for them. – *Star, Levanon, Ohio.*

❖ The adjective in "cheap politician" doesn't refer to what he costs the taxpayers – *Earl Wilson*

❖ Income taxes often transform nest eggs into goose eggs. – *Shannon Fife*

❖ Americans have come to believe that it's easier to vote for something they want than to work for it. – *H. C. Diefenbach*

❖ April 15 is the day when many a patriotic American feels bled-white and blue. – *Anna Herbert*

❖ The world situation is so mixed up because the wolves continue to ask for guarantees against attacks by the lambs. – *Celal Nasri*

❖ None of the evils which totalitarianism claims to remedy is worse than totalitarianism itself. – *Albert Camus*

❖ The biggest trouble with political promises is that they go in one year and out the other. – *Sylvia Bremer*

❖ Little things count, and three of them give you an $1,800 tax exemption – *Banking*

❖ A vicious circle—the present generation pays the bills of the last by issuing bonds for the next to pay.

❖ There'll be no tax on thinking. It would produce little revenue! – *K-Lens-M Komments* (September, 1963)

❖ It is reported that one bureaucrat said to another, "So we made a mistake. Don't just stand there. Label it a top secret and file it."

❖ It wasn't too long ago that you could finance a pretty good war for what six months of peace costs today. – *Bill Vaughan*

❖ When the time comes to vote, consider what a man has been— not what he promises to be.

❖ The trouble with China is the Confucian there. – *K-Lens-M Komments* (May, 1965)

❖ We always have lots of character assassination around election time; that's when politicians start shooting from the lip.

❖ People who spend all of their time demanding their rights seldom have time to take advantage of the privileges offered them.

❖ The unkindest cut of all is Uncle Sam's. – *Francis H. Bishop*

❖ Even better than disarmament as a step toward permanent peace might be some sort of international law that no new war could be started until all the books about the last one had been published. – *Bill Vaughan, Bell Syndicate*

❖ Take a look at your tax bills, and stop calling our lawmakers cheap politicians.

❖ Congress can legislate until doomsday, but the basis of our national prosperity is still an honest day's work.

❖ This is the only country where they lock up the jury and let the criminal go home every night.

❖ Wars and arguments have never solved the world's problems.

❖ In our nation's capital there are three great parties—Democratic, Republican, and Cocktail.

❖ America's greatest national resource is resourcefulness.
– *K-Lens-M Komments* (May, 1965)

❖ After November Election Day, many a politician who thought he was riding on the bandwagon realized that he was only on a dump cart.

❖ A dictator would have a tough time in a country like this, where the people would like to kill the umpire for making just one mistake.

❖ Someone once said, "There is one law for the rich and one for the poor." How lucky they are. Look at how many laws the rest of us have to obey.

❖ A crisis is an international incident that lasts long enough for us to locate it on the map. – *Bill Vaughan*

❖ The U.N. might test itself by disarming our juvenile delinquents.
– *K-Lens-M Komments* (August, 1965)

❖ It's the fiction in politics that causes most of the friction.

❖ One exercise too many Americans neglect is exercising their right to vote.

❖ It is true that people are born equal, but it takes constant practice to keep them that way.

❖ No amount of pay ever made a good soldier.

❖ Our new state, Hawaii, may send hula dancers to Congress because they know how to put motions before the house.

❖ We hope the scientists discover that Mars is not inhabited. This country can't afford to stretch foreign aid any further.

❖ All men may be born equal, but a great many refuse to stay in the class in which they were born.

❖ The huge national debt our younger generation will inherit should keep them from one indulgence—ancestor worship.
– *The Wall Street Journal*

❖ The government issues bulletins on doing away with all nuisances except foolish laws.

❖ The way to end wars will never be fought with guns.

❖ After going through a few global wars, all nations should have enough experience to believe in peace.

❖ About the only thing left nowadays to tax is one's memory.

❖ Two kinds of people work for the government: Civil servants who get sick leaves and pensions and taxpayers who don't.

❖ If Karl Marx were alive today, his problem would be to find parking spaces for the American proletariat rather than to break their chains of economic slavery. – *G. K. Reddy*

❖ In the welfare state it costs too much to get something for nothing.

❖ Every time politicians open their mouths they step on the gas. – *K-Lens-M Komments* (August, 1965)

❖ Said a little old lady to an income tax clerk, "I do hope you will give my money to a nice country."

❖ Capital punishment: spending the summer in Washington, D.C. – *Richard Armour*

❖ Nuclear war won't be a question of what's right, but rather what's left. – *Albert Savage*

❖ We've had the "New Deal" and the "Fair Deal." Some taxpayers are calling what we have now "The Ordeal."

❖ You really have to hand it to the income tax people—or they'll come after you.

❖ It's a very hard job today for an independent man to keep the government from taking care of him.

❖ The most serious impediment to marriage these days is the difficulty of supporting both a wife and the government on one income.

❖ When a politician changes his mind, it means he has either seen the light or felt the heat.

❖ United States Ambassador to the Soviet Union, "The two most ridiculous statements I know are 'Liquor doesn't affect me,' and 'I understand the Russians.'" – *Charles Bohlen*

❖ Our forefathers insured our freedom, but left it up to us to keep up the policy.

❖ Russian diplomat: an abominable no-man. – *Howard F Griffiths*

❖ The trouble with election jokes is that some of them get elected to office!

❖ It could be that what's wrong with the national economy is that there isn't any.

❖ Petition: a list of people who didn't have the nerve to say "no." – *The Sign*

❖ Income tax: guaranteed annual rage. – *Edwin Franks*

❖ A successful politician is one who can get in the public eye without irritating it. – *Vesta M. Kelly*

❖ The punishment wise men suffer for indifference to public affairs is to be ruled by unwise men.

❖ If you can keep your shirt on while getting something off your chest, you're a diplomat.

❖ The West, with all its natural beauty, was won by men on horseback—and is being lost to men on bulldozers. – *Harry Karns*

❖ The Vice Presidency is sort of like the last cookie on the plate. Everybody insists he won't take it, but somebody always does. – *Bill Vaughan*

❖ Every reform was once a private opinion. – *Ralph Waldo Emerson*

❖ Vote for the man who promises least; he'll be the least disappointing. – *Bernard Baruch*

❖ Peace, so far, has been just an interval between two wars.

❖ Most national leaders want to smoke the peace pipe, but none wants to inhale.

❖ This country is composed of two kinds of people. One group believes that the government can support all the citizens. The other wonders whether all the citizens can support the government.
– *James A. Farley*

❖ A great thing about living in this country is that we have complete control of how we pay our taxes—cash, check or money order.

❖ Trial by jury is something that every American believes in – until it comes time for him to serve on the jury. – *Shelley Berman*

❖ Today's diplomat is nothing more than a glorified horse-trader.

❖ Never judge a politician's thoughts by his remarks.

❖ No matter what other countries may say about us, immigration is the sincerest form of flattery. – *Pathfinder*

❖ Today's biggest sales problem is selling world peace.

❖ Psychologists believe that no person should keep too much to himself. And so does the Internal Revenue Service.
– *Floyd R. Miller*

❖ The birth of each new nation somehow finds Uncle Sam the babysitter. – *Shannon Fife*

❖ The more socialism we have in government, the higher our taxes will be, and the less social life we will have.

❖ Juvenile delinquent: a minor who is a major problem.
– *Arthur Murray*

❖ Trouble is there are too many Democratic and Republican Senators and not enough United States Senators. – *Ed Ford*

❖ Progress walks in Indian file behind a guy willing to stick his neck out. – *Bill Gold*

❖ In free countries, every man is entitled to express his opinions— and every other man is entitled not to listen. – *G. Norman Collie*

❖ The trouble with foreign affairs today is that you can never tell whether dictators are smart men bluffing or imbeciles who mean it. – *Automotive Dealer News*

❖ Cold war: nations flexing their missiles. – *Changing Times, The Kiplinger Magazine*

❖ Next to being shot at and missed, nothing is more gratifying than an income tax return.

❖ The reason modern folks don't appreciate freedom is because they don't know what it isn't.

❖ The world was created in six days, no Senate confirmation being necessary. – *Arkansas Gazette*

❖ There are plenty of hidden taxes today, but not one place for a taxpayer to hide.

❖ There are two forms of government—the short form and the long form. – *Look*

❖ The trouble with the public debt is that private individuals have to pay for it. – *Mary H. Waldrip*

❖ One reason why Rome wasn't built in a day was that it was a government job.

❖ Don't believe the communists will ever take over this country. They couldn't pay the taxes.

❖ This is the time of year when we all take a lot of capital punishment—income tax.

❖ Don't expect your rights to give you special privileges.

❖ If you think there ought to be a law, there probably is.

❖ People who don't take time to vote have no right to kick.

❖ Traffic cop: a stop-and-go getter. – *K-Lens-M Komments*

❖ Organized demonstration: trained zeal. – *H. E. Martz*

❖ We're thankful we have free speech in this country and equally thankful that there's no law requiring us to listen to it.

❖ Most people living in foreign lands seem to think our foreign policy is an endowment policy.

❖ Dictators seem to think the only way to have a well-ordered world is to let them give the orders.

❖ Past wars have left many displaced persons. Future wars are apt to leave many dispersoned places.

❖ The real destroyer of the liberties of any people is he who spreads among them bounties, donations and largess. – *Plutarch*

❖ California: a state that's washed by the Pacific on one side and cleaned by Las Vegas on the other. – *Earl Wilson*

❖ The trouble with America's foreign relations is that so many of them are broke. – *The Wall Street Journal*

❖ History reveals that most wars start in spring. Perhaps house-cleaning has something to do with this. – *K-Lens-M Komments* (May, 1964)

❖ The United States is the only country prosperous enough to make unemployment financially attractive.

❖ A taxpayer is one who doesn't have to pass a civil service examination to work for the government.

❖ Only in a free country are people allowed to kick because they don't think it is.

❖ At Eskimo trial: "Where were you the night of October 11 to April 3?"

❖ Perfect poise: looking unconcerned when a tax investigator checks your return. – *K-Lens-M Komments* (April, 1964)

❖ The type of man who robs Peter to pay Paul usually causes both of them to suffer.

❖ Most of the people who talk the loudest about capital and labor never had any capital and never did any labor.

❖ If some people got their rights, they would complain of being deprived of their wrongs. – *Oliver Herford*

❖ True security never runs smooth. – *K-Lens-M Komments* (May, 1965)

❖ There's this to be said about the average taxpayer: he's alive—and kicking. – *Vesta M. Kelly*

❖ A communist is a fellow who likes what he doesn't have so much that he doesn't want you to have it either.

❖ Freedom of speech was arranged by ancestors who had no idea of what was going to be said.

❖ A sure sign of bureaucracy is when the first person who answers the phone can't help you. – *Kenneth J. Fabian, M.D.*

❖ Perhaps a tax break would help some of us to break even.
– *K-Lens-M Komments* (March, 1964)

❖ Government has to be cut back like asparagus, every day, or it gets away and goes to seed. – *Paul Harvey*

❖ It is not the function of our government to keep the citizens from falling into error; it is the function of the citizen to keep the government from falling into error. – *Justice Robert H. Jackson*

❖ Despite what the cartoonists make him look like, Uncle Sam is a gentleman with a very large waste.

❖ A deficit is usually all that remains after the bottom falls out of good intentions.

❖ The next president is increasing in numbers. – *K-Lens-M Komments* (March, 1964)

❖ Federal aid is giving yourself a transfusion by drawing blood from your right arm, returning it to your left—and spilling 90 percent on the way across. – *Modern Medicine*

❖ What the average community needs are public servants young enough to serve, old enough to know better, and good enough to be honest.

❖ We have two political parties—not because there are two sides to every question, but because there are two sides to every office—the outside and the inside.

❖ Atlas supported the world, they say, but he had no income tax to pay! – *K-Lens-M Komments*

❖ Politics is a game in which some men are self-made but most are machine-made. – *Democrat & Chronicle*

❖ Welfare state: where it costs too much to get something for nothing. – *K-Lens-M Komments* (March, 1964)

❖ Every word that a president says weighs a ton. – *Calvin Coolidge*

❖ Some income tax refunds seem slower than a helicopter over a nudist camp. – *K-Lens-M Komments* (July, 1964)

❖ Our generation was brought up on the wrong side of the tax. – *The Wall Street Journal*

❖ The toughest part of politics is to satisfy the voter without giving him what he wants. – *Dan Bennett*

❖ Why don't they cut taxes like bikinis? – *K-Lens-M Komments* (October, 1963)

❖ It appears that we're sending arms to just about everybody but the Venus de Milo. – *Fletcher Knebel*

❖ I favor the policy of the economy, not because I wish to save money, but because I wish to save people. – *Calvin Coolidge*

❖ Presidential candidate handshaking provides enough energy to milk all the taxpayers for four years. – *K-Lens-M Komments* (May, 1964)

❖ Men are really patriotic when they are called to serve on a jury in a bathing beauty contest.

❖ Hidden taxes are hidden no better than hidden charms.
  – *K-Lens-M Komments* (October, 1963)

❖ Drill sergeant to recruit: "Wipe that opinion off your face!"
  – *Bennett Emerson*

❖ Pentagon: building with five sides—on every issue. – *In a Nutshell*

❖ If history happens to repeat itself again in this atomic age, it may make a long story short. – *K-Lens-M Komments*

❖ It is regrettable that, among the Rights of Man, the right of contradicting oneself has been forgotten. – *Baudelaire*

❖ Statesman: politician who's been dead 10 or 15 years.
  – *Harry S. Truman*

❖ Some of the fences politicians are trying to mend are made of live wire. – *K-Lens-M Komments* (April, 1964)

❖ It's easy enough to enact laws with teeth in them, but few have wisdom teeth.

❖ In many countries our embassies are only a stone's throw away.
  – *Pipe Lines*

❖ From a will: "And to my communist nephew, Oswald, I leave the sum of ten thousand pounds—to be shared equally with his fellow Britishers." – *John Carpenter*

❖ The diplomat who doesn't know what to say has learned that it is better to say so.

❖ Keeping the peace is like winning a war—it calls for straight shooting. – *K–Lens–M Komments* (August, 1964)

❖ Washington: the city bureauful. – *G. C. Ebbert*

Surprising Facts by K-Lens-M Komments

✓ China used war rockets 1,500 B.C. (September, 1963)
✓ U.S. presidents sign their name about 160,000 times a year. (July, 1964)
✓ The government owns 1/3 of the total U.S. land area. (May, 1965)

Happiness

❖ Write it on your heart that every day is the best day of the year.
  – *R. W. Emerson*

❖ People who have little and want less are far happier than those who have much and want more.

❖ Worry is the interest paid on trouble long before the principal becomes due.

❖ An optimist laughs to forget, while a pessimist forgets to laugh.

❖ Pessimists not only expect the worst, but go out to meet it.

❖ Some people are never happy unless they have something to be mad about.

❖ True happiness comes to the person who gets something he wanted but did not expect.

❖ Give your worries a little time and they'll settle themselves.

❖ Keep smiling. It makes everyone wonder what you've been up to.

❖ The optimist is he who sees a light that is not there; the pessimist is the foolish one who is trying to blow it out.

❖ Sympathy is never wasted except when you give it to yourself.
  – *John W. Raper*

❖ You are genuinely happy if you don't know why. – *Joseph Mayer*

❖ Smiles cost much less than electric lights, but they make the home brighter.

❖ A lot of people who have nothing wrong with them forget to let their faces know about it.

❖ The best way to cheer yourself up is to cheer everybody else up. – *Mark Twain*

❖ Pessimistic people manage to dodge a lot of good things that are headed their way.

❖ When you worry, you are paying interest on nothing.

❖ Even though you may have no reason to smile, it's a good idea to keep in practice anyway.

❖ A pessimist is a fellow who resents the fact that the world was made without asking his advice.

❖ The man who is too busy making good to nurse a grouch is on the road to real happiness.

❖ Half the people of the world are unhappy because they don't have the things that make the other half miserable.

❖ A pessimist greatly fears his worst fears won't be realized.

❖ The unhappy are always wrong—wrong in being so, wrong in saying so, and wrong in making others so.

❖ Worry is like a rocking chair; it gives you something to do, but it won't get you anyplace.

❖ How comforting it is to know that less than half the trouble people figure on never comes.

❖ Why worry about the things you can't control? Get busy controlling the things that depend on you.

❖ One good way to test your memory is to try to remember the things that worried you yesterday. – *Toronto Star*

❖ If you feel good today, be sure to let your face know it.

❖ An optimist is a man who is just starting to shovel out a long driveway; a pessimist is one who has been working at it for five minutes. – *Contributed by Richard Attridge*

❖ You can't expect to live in a sunny world if you're wearing a cloud on your brow.

❖ Unhappiness is in not knowing what we want and killing ourselves to get it. – *Don Herold*

❖ The secret of happiness sometimes depends on what you don't do.

❖ I make it a rule always to believe compliments implicitly for five minutes, and to simmer gently for twenty more. – *Alice James, quoted in Christian Herald*

❖ Worry is a useless old reprobate who comes too early or too late. – *K-Lens-M Komments* (October, 1965)

❖ Morale is when your hands and feet keep on working when your head says it can't be done. – *Admiral Ben Moreell, quoted in Forbes*

❖ The most completely lost of all days is the one during which you did not laugh.

❖ Grief can take care of itself, but to get the full value of joy, you must have someone to share it with. – *Mark Twain*

❖ A pessimist is a guy who thinks life is a game of tag—and he is always it.

❖ One ought every day to hear a little music, read a good poem, see a fine picture, and if possible, speak a few reasonable words.
– *Goethe*

❖ Making life easier doesn't seem to make people happier.
– *K-Lens-M Komments* (October, 1963)

❖ Success is getting what you want. Happiness is wanting what you get.

❖ Every minute you are angry, you lose sixty seconds of pleasure.

❖ If a man doesn't get happier as he grows older, he hasn't learned what he should along the way.

❖ There will come a time when every man is contented with his lot—when he is buried in it.

❖ Neurotic: a person who worries about things that didn't happen in the past—instead of worrying about something that won't happen in the future, like normal people.

❖ If anything gets under our hide, it's locking our car with the keys inside. – *K-Lens-M Komments* (August, 1964)

❖ People who dodge the problems of life sometimes have less to worry about than those who try to solve them.

❖ Worry is as useless as whispering in a boiler factory.

❖ It is not what one does for people, but the way one makes them feel that shapes their happiness.

❖ It pays to preserve your peace of mind—it's the only peace that you can find. – *K-Lens-M Komments* (May, 1965)

❖ He who spends all his time hating his enemies misses chances to do many more useful things.

❖ Too much foresight causes many a man to worry about things that never happen.

❖ Worry: putting today's sun under tomorrow's cloud.

❖ Some people lose the first part of their lives to make themselves unhappy for the second part.

❖ If you don't intend to do anything about it, worry is very silly. If you do really intend to do something about it, worry isn't necessary.

❖ Wear a frown and have wrinkles; wear a smile and have friends.

❖ Much happiness is overlooked because it doesn't cost anything.

❖ The dove of peace is with us still, but we see nothing but the gill!

❖ Telling our troubles can leave us sad; some folks aren't sorry—others are glad. – *K-Lens-M Komments*

❖ Pretensions are a source of pain, and the happy time of life begins as soon as we give them up. – *Nicolas Chamfort*

❖ To worry about the past is to reopen a grave; let the corpse alone. To worry about the future is to dig your own grave. Let the undertaker do that.

❖ If you want to be continuously happy, you must know when to be blind, when to be deaf, and when to be dumb.

❖ Look beyond your troubles and you'll see the sunshine.

❖ Happiness seldom comes to those who try to live on the spice of life.

❖ Worry admitted as a guest soon becomes the head of the house. – *K-Lens-M Komments* (August, 1964)

❖ Doctors say that to stay healthy, be happy. It seems that it's the surly bird that catches the germ.

❖ A sense of humor is what lets you laugh at something that would have made you mad had it happened to you.

❖ It is the growling man who lives a dog's life.

❖ Cheerfulness: window cleaner of the mind. – *K-Lens-M Komments*

❖ Stop fretting over things that can't be helped, and go do the things that can be done.

❖ More people die from worry than from work; so work hard and have less time to worry.

❖ Pessimist: usually a man who financed an optimist. – *F. G. Kiernan*

❖ If it were as easy to arouse enthusiasm as it is suspicion, just think what could be accomplished.

❖ The guy who said there was no use crying over spilled milk probably only paid six cents a quart.

❖ If happiness could really be bought, lots of folks would grumble about the price and the rest couldn't raise the down payment.

❖ Enjoy yourself—it really pays; these are tomorrow's good old days. – *K-Lens-M Komments*

❖ If ignorance is bliss, it's amazing there aren't more happy people.

❖ Pessimists are just average people who can't kid themselves.

❖ An optimist is wrong as often as a pessimist, but he has a lot more fun.

❖ The worst thing about crossing a bridge before you get to it is that it leaves you on this side of the river.

❖ Optimist: one who thinks things can't get much worse. – *K-Lens-M Komments* (June, 1962)

❖ Worry is like running away from something that isn't after you.

❖ The pleasure of what we enjoy is lost by coveting more.

❖ Hurry is the visible form of worry. – *K-Lens-M Komments* (August, 1965)

❖ He who is too easily carried away with enthusiasm usually has to walk back.

❖ When I go to bed, I leave my troubles in my clothes.

❖ It takes thirteen facial muscles to smile and forty-seven to frown. But a lot of people evidently don't mind the extra muscular activity, for they walk around looking nasty and glum. They don't realize that they are neglecting one of their most attractive assets. – *James Bender and Lee Graham*

❖ The cost of everything has gone up but happiness; smiles and kind words are as cheap as ever.

❖ You can't have your cake and somebody else's cookie, too.
 – *K-Lens-M Komments* (October, 1965)

❖ Happiness is the reward the world bestows on people who have learned how to live.

❖ The man who gets along best is he who can look happy when he isn't.

❖ Dark and gloomy days are unknown to people who have learned to spread sunshine.

❖ A pessimist is one who feels bad when he feels good, for fear he will feel worse tomorrow.

❖ An optimist hopes for the best and makes the most of what he gets.

❖ The man with smiles to lend has no reason to borrow trouble.

❖ He who can bottle up a little sunshine for a rainy day is a corker.

❖ If you'd like to be happy, here is the way: don't live tomorrow until you've lived today.

❖ Of all the things you wear, your expression is the most important.
 – *Janet Lane*

❖ He who is never satisfied with anything satisfies no one.

❖ The harvest of happiness is most often reaped through the hands of helpfulness.

❖ A pessimist is just a sentimental optimist who expected too much.

❖ Pessimist: misfortune teller. – *K-Lens-M Komments*

❖ Hope is a good breakfast, but a bad supper. – *English Proverb*

❖ The pursuit of happiness gives some folks the chase of a lifetime.

❖ Happiness is a homemade article.

❖ Worry: weak substitute for thinking. – *K-Lens-M Komments*

Worry Warts — *Author unknown*
Living is so complicated these days, folks don't even worry right.
For instance:
We worry about the Russians, then get run over by a neighbor's car.
We worry about radioactive fallout, then get poisoned by nicotine or by spraying the flowers.
We worry about the youngsters running in front of cars, then drag them across the street against the warning of the red light.
We worry about crashing in an airplane, then fall off a ladder painting the house.
We worry about getting enough exercise, then drive two blocks for a cup of coffee.
We worry about getting the car greased every thousand miles, then never get a medical checkup.
We worry about retirement, then go about carelessly to keep from lasting that long.
We worry about H-bombs, then blow our heads off by smoking around gasoline.
We worry about polio, then get crippled by running into a power lawn mower.
We worry about tornadoes, then get liquidated in a traffic accident.

Health

* Ulcers are caused not so much by what you eat as by what's eating you.

* The amount of sleep required by the average person is just five minutes more.

* Insomnia can be caused by many things, but very seldom by things a man didn't say.

* The worst case of insomnia on record is that of the man who could not sleep even when it was time to get up.

* The horridest of horror tales is sometimes told by the bathroom scales. – *Eunice Landfield in Successful Farming Magazine*

* For some people, the best time of the day is over when the alarm clock rings.

* Even when only one person has it, rheumatism is a joint affair.

* Some of us attain our ends by not exercising enough. – *K-Lens-M Komments* (October, 1963)

* Walking is the best exercise, if you can dodge those who aren't. – *Herbert V. Prochnow*

* A cold can be both positive and negative—the eyes and the nose can have it at the same time.

❖ Many a hypochondriac suffers from symptoms for which there's no disease. – *K-Lens-M Komments* (September, 1963)

❖ A psychiatrist is a man who charges you so much to tell you to get away from it all that you can't afford to take the trip.

❖ About 15,000,000 Americans have poor hearing and the rest won't listen. – *K-Lens-M Komments* (July, 1964)

❖ Practical nurse: one who marries a rich patient. – *Martha Raye*

❖ The best way to keep healthy is to eat what you don't want, drink what you don't like, and do what you'd rather not.

❖ Bad health is usually a cure for bad habits!

❖ Specialist: a doctor whose patients are expected to confine their ailments to office hours. – *T. J. McInerney*

❖ The best doctor is the one you run for and can't find.

❖ Chiropodist: a man who makes money hand over foot.
– *Mrs. C. B. Thomas*

❖ When the temperature is minus, I feel it in my sinus.
– *Bill Vaughan*

❖ Her ailments are psychodramatic. – *Tom Pease*

❖ Miracle drug: one you can get the children to take. – *K-Lens-M Komments* (September, 1963)

❖ Isn't it strange that they've had to build hospitals in every town since those old-fashioned grandmother's remedies went out of fashion?

❖ The best place for an overweight person to put a mirror is on the door of the refrigerator.

❖ They say germs have billions of relatives. It serves 'em right! – *K-Lens-M Komments*

❖ A generation ago, most men who finished a day's work needed rest; now they need exercise. – *General Features Corp.*

❖ Pain: nature's policeman. – *K-Lens-M Komments* (August, 1964)

❖ When friends tell you how to cure a sore throat, take it with a grain of salt. The salt may do some good. – *Herald Post, El Paso, Texas*

❖ Cough: something you yourself can't help, but everybody else does on purpose to torment you. – *Ogden Nash*

❖ Nobody is sicker than the man who is sick on his day off. – *Bill Vaughan*

❖ Life for stout men has its sad side; they can't run and they can't hide. – *K-Lens-M Komments* (August, 1965)

❖ Said a local physician to a patient, "Let me know if this prescription works. I'm having the same trouble myself."

❖ There's no such thing as the common cold—ours are always uncommon. – *K-Lens-M Komments*

❖ A local doctor told a patient, "That check you gave me for my last visit, came back." Came the instant reply, "Sorry, Doc, but so did my arthritis."

❖ Sign in a nearby small drug store: "Buy our cough syrup. You will never get any better."

❖ I reckon being ill is one of the great pleasures of life, provided one is not too ill and is not obliged to work till one is better. – *Samuel Butler*

❖ Chapped lips aren't all they're cracked up to be.

❖ Nothing breeds fatigue like inactivity. – *O. A. Battista*

❖ The best place for your bathroom scales is in front of your refrigerator. – *Imogene Fey in The Saturday Evening Post*

❖ Psychiatric examination: a check-up from the neck up. – *Richard Wheeler*

❖ A smile a day keeps the psychiatrist away. – *K-Lens-M Komments* (April, 1964)

❖ Fortunately psychoanalysis is not the only way to resolve inner conflicts. Life itself still remains a very effective therapist. – *Dr. Karen Horney, Our Inner Conflicts*

❖ A smile is contagious, yet it is recommended by the Board of Health.

❖ Walking is good for the health if you can manage to keep out of the way of automobiles.

❖ Overweight is the only problem that's worse after it's settled – *A. David Griffith*

❖ About all the exercise a lot of people get is pulling ice trays from the refrigerator. – *K-Lens-M Komments*

❖ Virus is a Latin word used by doctors to mean "your guess is as good as mine." – *Bob Hope*

❖ Walking reduces weight; jaywalking reduces years.

❖ Blessed are the deaf. They do not hear the yakking of the dumb.

❖ The two most important muscles operating without the direction of the brain are the heart and the tongue. – *K-Lens-M Komments*

❖ Figures come all shapes and sorts, but many come too big for shorts. – *Elinor K. Rose*

❖ Then there was the fellow who was so thin that a backache and a stomachache hit him in the same place.

❖ Overweight: just desserts. – *In a Nutshell*

❖ Early to bed and early to rise is a habit that most folks despise. – *K-Lens-M Komments* (August, 1963)

❖ I've lost my glasses and I can't look for them until I find them.

❖ Ulcers are something you get from mountain climbing over molehills.

❖ Definition of a psychiatrist: one who will tell you that you are crazy and you pay him twenty-five dollars for his opinion, which proves you are.

❖ Psychiatrist: a man who doesn't have to worry as long as other people do. – *Chal Herry*

❖ Anyone who can swallow an aspirin tablet at a drinking fountain deserves to get well.

❖ Hope and sleep are the best tranquilizers. – *K-Lens-M Komments*

❖ Arthritis: twinges in the hinges. – *G. B. Howard*

❖ You can't fly with the owls at night and keep up with the eagles in the daytime.

❖ It is now proved beyond doubt that smoking is one of the leading causes of statistics. – *Fletcher Knebel*

Out on a Limerick *by Bennett Cerf*

There was a young man with a hernia
Who said to his doctor, "Gol dernia,
When improving my middle
Be sure you don't fiddle
With matters that do not concernia."
— *Heywood Brown*

Surprising Facts by K-Lens-M Komments

✓ Opium was the aspirin of ancient Egypt. (May, 1963)
✓ Every year, one out of seven Americans seeks hospital care. (August, 1963)
✓ About 68 cents of every dollar paid for hospital services in the U. S. goes for salaries. (August, 1963)
✓ Most of us hear better with our left ear. (October, 1963)
✓ Man's life expectancy has almost doubled in the past hundred years. (March, 1964)
✓ Your sense of smell is keener at night. (April, 1964)
✓ Gout is found most frequently in business executives. (May, 1964)
✓ Twice as many girls as boys have asthma. (July, 1964)
✓ The Egyptians used toothbrushes in 1620 B.C. (July, 1964)
✓ Americans take about 16,000,000,000 aspirin tablets a year. (May, 1965)
✓ Men are 30 percent more restless in their sleep. (August, 1965)
✓ Drug stores offer 1,200 cold remedies. (October, 1965)

Hobbies & Sports

❖ A hobby is something you get goofy about to keep from going nuts about things in general.

❖ Rock 'n' Roll music: earitation

❖ The trouble with golf is that by the time you can afford to lose a ball, you can't hit it that far. – *Marty Allen in New York Mirror*

❖ Skier: a person with a two-track mind. – *K-Lens-M Komments*

❖ The football season is when you watch the numbers on sweaters instead of in 'em.

❖ When a habit begins to cost a lot of money, it is called a hobby.

❖ Another man who must be good at handling figures is a ballet dancer. – *K-Lens-M Komments* (August, 1965)

❖ The hardest thing about skating is the ice, when you come right down to it. – *Boys' Life*

❖ No matter how the college alumni travel to the game, they all end up riding the coach. – *Earl Wilson*

❖ You needn't be clever at card tricks to make the Jack disappear. – *K-Lens-M Komments* (May, 1964)

❖ If you think it's hard to meet new people, pick up the wrong golf ball. – *The Wall Street Journal*

❖ Football season: when fall bills kick Dad for a goal.
– *K-Lens-M Komments* (October, 1963)

❖ It is fine to learn dancing from Arthur Murray, but it's a lot more fun dancing with a girl.

❖ Hobby: voluntary work. – *K-Lens-M Komments*

❖ Skiing is best when you have lots of white snow and plenty of Blue Cross. – *Earl Wilson*

❖ On skiing: By the time I learned to stand up, I couldn't sit down. – *Robert Q. Lewis*

❖ Old stamp collectors never die—they just trade away.

❖ Most of man's inventions have been timesavers—then came television. – *Joe Ryan, Ben Roth Syndicate*

❖ Football: windbag. – *K-Lens-M Komments*

❖ Some novels you just can't put down; others you don't dare to if there are children in the house.

❖ To dance the "Twist" we will not stoop—it's hula hoop without the hoop. – *K-Lens-M Komments*

❖ We read recently that post card collectors are called deltiologists. After all, they have to be called something.

❖ Uncle Sam's hobby is coin collecting. – *K-Lens-M Komments* (October, 1965)

❖ The trouble with portable television is that you can take it with you. – *Homer Phillips*

❖ Tennis racket: a bunch of holes strung together.

❖ The hobby that makes sense is weeding out your worries.
    – *K-Lens-M Komments* (October, 1963)

❖ Golf is a ball. I drive it down the middle in true, unerring flight.
    Then I try to solve a riddle: just what did I do right?
    – *Eugene McAllister*

❖ A downtown lady told us her husband doesn't play cards for
    money but those who play with him do.

❖ Teetotaler: a golfer disputing your score. – *K-Lens-M Komments*
    (August, 1965)

❖ Golf is a great diversion. It helps people save their health and lose
    their temper.

❖ A football coach's toughest problems are defensive linebackers
    and offensive alumni.

❖ Winning isn't everything unless a coach likes to keep his job.
    – *K-Lens-M Komments* (September, 1963)

❖ Early to bed and early to rise is a sure sign that you are fed up
    with television.

❖ If your nerves are throbby, it's time to find a hobby.
    – *K-Lens-M Komments* (August, 1964)

❖ Television is a medium of entertainment that permits millions of
    people to listen to the same joke at the same time and yet remain
    lonesome. – *T. S. Eliot*

❖ A golf ball should be hit every time—but not too often.
    – *K-Lens-M Komments* (July, 1964)

❖ In Africa, native tribes beat the ground with clubs and utter blood-curdling yells. Anthropologists call this primitive self-expression. Here we call it golf.

❖ A football field is one place it pays to kick when things aren't going well. – *K-Lens-M Komments* (September, 1963)

❖ Adults who do the twist should remember their age. Youngsters who do the twist should behave.

❖ Don't believe the tales that golfers tell; the ball lies poorly—the players lie well. – *K-Lens-M Komments* (June, 1962)

❖ Horse racing is a clean sport. It cleans thousands of people every day.

❖ Most incomplete forward passes are made to cute cheerleaders. – *K-Lens-M Komments* (October, 1963)

❖ Tee Time: a well-adjusted person is one who can play golf and bridge as if they were games. – *Chicago Tribune*

❖ Some feminine skaters are easy on the ice. – *K-Lens-M Komments*

❖ Sponsors: people who make television programs possible and impossible at the same time. – *Dan Bennett*

❖ Polo: sophisticated horseplay. – *K-Lens-M Komments* (August, 1965)

❖ Golf is a lot of walking, broken up by disappointments and bad arithmetic. – *Earl Wilson*

❖ A racetrack is the only place with windows that clean people.

❖ What a dancer needs most is a good head on his shoulder. – *K-Lens-M Komments* (March, 1964)

❖ An auction is where, if you're not careful, you'll get something for nodding. – *Town Journal*

Surprising Facts by K-Lens-M Komments

✓ A golf ball travels over 100 miles an hour. (June, 1962)
✓ It is spelled jujitsu. (June, 1962)
✓ Fast sprinters run about 20 mph. (June, 1962)
✓ The earth's rotation has an effect on thrown objects (June, 1962)
✓ 50,000,000 U.S. adults read comic strips. (August, 1963)
✓ About 6,000,000 Americans engage in water skiing (September, 1963)
✓ The world surf casting record is over 700 ft. (September, 1963)
✓ Bowling pins vary in weight. (September, 1963)
✓ Football players are active about one-tenth of playing time. (October, 1963)
✓ Playing cards are 1,000 years old. We have played with that deck! (October, 1965)

Holidays

❖ Santa Claus has the right idea—visit people once a year.
  – Earl Wilson

❖ Christmas shopping: the only suitable gift for the man who has everything is your deepest sympathy. *– Imogene Fey*

❖ What the world needs is more mistletoe and less missile talk.
  – Paul J. Santee

❖ The best gift of all: the presence of a happy family all wrapped up in each other.

❖ Some people's idea of celebrating the holidays is to have a Christmas they'll never forget and a New Year's Eve they can't remember.

❖ One of our present troubles seems to be that too many adults, and not enough children, believe in Santa Claus.
  – The New Orleans Blue Book

❖ At Christmas, what the kids would like is something that will separate the men from the toys. *– Byjac News*

❖ When the leaves begin to fall, then 'til Christmas is no time at all. *– K-Lens-M Komments* (October, 1963)

❖ This is the time of year when every contract between parent and child has a Santa clause in it. *– Jack E. Leonard*

❖ A father's biggest difficulty at Christmastime is convincing the children that he is Santa Claus, and his wife that he isn't.
– *Bill Ireland*

❖ A harried mother says, "At Christmastime the kids hang up their stockings. After that it's a full year before any of them hangs up anything again." – *Roger Allen*

❖ The Christmas holidays can be divided into four periods: anticipation, preparation, prostration and recuperation.

❖ There's nothing so shopworn as a last-minute Christmas shopper.
– *Al Magee*

❖ What this country needs is a New Year's resolution that will pay Christmas bills.

Humor

❖ Let's cross electric blankets with toasters and pop people out of bed.

❖ A chrysanthemum by any other name would at least be easier to spell.

❖ Give an athlete an inch and he'll take a foot. But let him take it. Who wants athlete's foot, anyway?

❖ We like to hear people laugh, but not when we are chasing our hat down the street.

❖ Sign in a department store window: "Bath towels for the whole damp family."

❖ They're called cuckoo clocks because they keep tocking to themselves.

❖ Television will never replace the newspaper. Just try swatting a fly with a TV set.

❖ If you knew the editor was going to tell the absolute truth in your obituary, what would you quit doing now? — *Citizen, Utah*

❖ Had an awful scare last night. I turned on my radio set by mistake and thought I'd gone blind! – *Kay Kyser*

❖ Cousin Helen is so fussy she exchanged her gift certificates. – *K-Lens-M Komments*

❖ Disneyland is the greatest people trap in the world ever built by a mouse. – *Robert Cahn*

❖ A man stuck his neck in a noose to see if it would work. It did.

❖ Breathes there a man with soul so dead, who never to himself has said, "@#$%&*" as he stubbed his toe on the foot of the bed. – *E. K. Banfill*

❖ A tuba player wore a toupee. One night it slipped off and fell into his tuba. He spent the rest of the night blowing his top.

❖ Early to bed and early to rise will convince your friends that your TV is out of order.

❖ "That's enough out of you," said the surgeon as he sewed up his patient.

❖ Then there was the cowboy whose horse stopped suddenly— Injun trouble.

❖ Sign in a Muskogee, Oklahoma, restaurant: "If you is broke, you has done et."

❖ Uncle Homer says he feels as down and out as an unemployed elevator operator. – *K-Lens-M Komments*

❖ A man was going down the street in a barrel. A policeman asked, "Are you a poker player?" He replied, "No, but I just left some fellows who are."

❖ A rich Texas oilman has three swimming pools on his huge estate. One is filled with hot water, one with cold water, and one he keeps empty for his guests who don't swim.

❖ Natives who beat drums to drive off evil spirits are objects of scorn to smart American motorists who blow horns to break up traffic jams. – *Mary Ellen Kelly*

❖ A nervous passenger asked, "Captain, do ships like this often sink?" The skipper replied, "No, madam, only once."

❖ Humorist's epitaph: wit's end. – *K-Lens-M Komments* (August, 1964)

❖ There was a millionaire who spent so much money on his girl that he finally married her for his money.

❖ Sign in restaurant: "Use your fingers. Emily Post wouldn't eat here anyway."

❖ Parking place: a space occupied by someone already there. – *K-Lens-M Komments*

❖ In antique shop: "Come in and buy what your grandmother threw away." – *Mrs. Robert G. Williams*

❖ He who laughs last probably intended to tell the story himself. – *The Irish Digest*

❖ Some of these movies on TV are so old that they show bandits driving up in front of the bank—and finding a parking spot. – *Bill Vaughan*

❖ San Francisco's Chinatown telephone book lists 257 Wong numbers. – *Herb Caen*

❖ When pigeonholes hold pigeons and dovetails grow on doves, then look in the glove compartments for gloves. – *Penny Pennington*

❖ Is it worse to simmer in summer or to wither in winter?

Timeless Teachings from Mrs. Stroupe's Blackboard

– *K-Lens-M Komments* (August, 1963)

❖ Out in Texas, a widow told a friend that her late husband had been most unfortunate all his life, but that things had changed at the end. They struck oil when they dug his grave.

❖ The height of conceit: sending your mother a letter of congratulations on your own birthday.

❖ We heard of a bell-ringer who got tangled up in his rope and tolled himself off.

❖ Humor isn't humor without a grain of truth. – *K-Lens-M Komments* (September, 1963)

❖ Antique: a fugitive from the junkyard with a price on its head. – *Kenneth J. Shively*

❖ Then there was a dear old lady who had wheels put on her rocking chair so she could rock and roll.

❖ The question is how the ancient Egyptians were able to build the pyramids. In those days there were no wage or hour laws, no paid vacations nor coffee breaks.

❖ Smoke and the world smokes with you; swear off and you smoke alone. – *K-Lens-M Komments*

❖ A tree surgeon's son wanted to go into the business in a small way, so he opened a branch office.

❖ A local store has a cross-eyed detective, so people can't tell whom he is watching.

❖ A local wise guy went into a shoe store and asked, "How much are your twenty-dollar shoes?" A sharp clerk replied, "Ten dollars a foot."

❖ At the side of the road a woman looked helplessly at a flat tire. A passerby stopped to help. After they had changed the tire, the woman said, "Please let the jack down easy. My husband is asleep in the back seat."

❖ Extemporaneous jokes are hardest to memorize. – *K-Lens-M Komments* (September, 1963)

❖ A grain of sand in the shoe demands far more attention than a boulder beside the road.

❖ On a cereal box: "To open on dotted line, follow these seven easy steps." – *Steve Bliss*

❖ After reading the epitaphs in a cemetery, we wonder where they buried all the sinners.

❖ TV set: a watching machine. – *K-Lens-M Komments*

❖ Then there was the Texan who wrote a check and the bank bounced.

❖ You'll never be too busy to attend your own funeral.
– *K-Lens-M Komments*

❖ There are three things not worth running for—a bus, a woman, or a new economic panacea. If you wait a bit, another one will come along. – *Derick Heathcoat Amory, Britain's Chancellor of the Exchequer*

❖ A local girl told us that her sweetheart not only lied to her about his yacht, but made her do the rowing.

❖ The man who manufacturers woolen underwear irritates a lot of people.

❖ Mary had a bathing suit; it was very airy. Five percent was bathing suit; all the rest was Mary.

❖ On a newly opened diner: "Hopen for Business."
   – *Kenneth J. Holland*

❖ Joke book: jest seller. – *K-Lens-M Komments* (August, 1965)

❖ Too far east is west.

❖ Parking spaces, every time, never head the same way I'm.
   – *Lois F. Pasley*

❖ The difference between the old dime novel and the best seller of today is about $3.40.

❖ A man who can stand on his own feet is always admired in an elevator.

❖ If you can't locate a tree surgeon at his office, you may find him at one of his branches.

❖ A traveling salesman told a local waitress one morning, "Bring me two eggs fried so hard they are edged in black, two slices of burnt toast and a cup of cold coffee. Then sit down and nag me— I'm homesick."

❖ Don't boast of your ability until you have successfully folded a batch of road maps.

❖ A waiter's tipical smile. – *Bertha L. Goodwin*

❖ The alarm clock has been called the world's greatest uplifter.

❖ Oh, for the good old days when you could get the landlord to fix anything just by threatening to move.

❖ Needed: a soap that will prevent a telephone ring in the bathtub.
  – *K-Lens-M Komments*

❖ A new soap removes the ring from the tub. Now if they'll take
  the ring out of the phone, we can relax in our bath.

Out on a Limerick *by Bennett Cerf*

There was a young lady from Trent
Whose TV antenna got bent.
The neighbors went crazy,
Their screens all got hazy
For instead of receiving, she sent!
— *John Etheridge*

A certain young lady named Hanna
Was caught in a flood in Montannah.
As she floated away,
Her beau, so they say,
Accompanied her on the piannah.
— *Unknown*

There was a young girl from St. Paul
Who wore a newspaper dress to a ball.
But the dress caught on fire
And burned her entire
Front page—sporting section—and all.
— *Unknown*

Kindness & Politeness

Hearts, like doors, open with ease
To very, very little keys;
And don't forget that two are these:
"I thank you, Sir," and "If you please." – A. U.

❖ If you must slander someone, don't speak it, write it—in the sand near the water's edge.

❖ Forgetfulness may be due less to absentmindedness than to absent-heartedness. – *K-Lens-M Komments* (October, 1965)

❖ People who aim to please don't have to take time out for target practice.

❖ It may be true that one good turn deserves another, but there is no such thing as perpetual motion.

❖ One of life's greatest pleasures is to do a good deed in secret and then have it discovered by accident.

❖ Want to break the ice? Crack a smile.

❖ Small deeds done are better than great deeds planned.
– *Peter Marshall*

❖ The best way to enjoy regular dividends is to invest in courtesy.

❖ Compliments are not always genuine, but faultfinding addicts are always sincere.

❖ You have not fulfilled every duty unless you have fulfilled that of being pleasant.

❖ Kind acts are stepping stones to contentment and happiness.

❖ It takes a good sprinter to keep pace with his good intentions.

❖ A man cannot hold another down without stooping.

❖ Smile: a curve that will straighten out anything.

❖ If you sow a little kindness, you will reap a crop of friends.

❖ Courtesy and good manners often succeed where the best language has failed.

❖ Gratitude: memory of the heart. – *K-Lens-M Komments* (August, 1963)

❖ When you are being criticized, remember, sticks and stones are thrown only at fruit-bearing trees.

❖ If your ship fails to come in, it's time to get busy and help the other fellow unload his.

❖ As we survey the human scene, we find more people kind than mean.

❖ In spite of the high cost of everything, it costs nothing to pay a compliment occasionally.

❖ The best time for a kind deed is right now. – *K-Lens-M Komments* (October, 1965)

❖ Few of us get dizzy from doing too many good turns.

❖ Flowers leave part of their fragrance on the hand that bestows them.

❖ The person who delays writing a letter until in the mood usually expects a reply by return mail.

❖ A good rule as we go through life is to keep the heart softer than the head.

❖ The kindness planned for tomorrow doesn't count today. – *John M. Henry*

❖ Who gives to me teaches me to give.

❖ He who has had a personal introduction to misfortune seldom laughs at the misfortune of others.

❖ On a telephone truck in Oakland, California: "Courtesy is contagious; let's start an epidemic."

❖ Kindness is another form of riches that cannot be taxed.

❖ Courtesy costs not a cent and pays off in real dollars.

❖ Kindness: charm within reach of all. – *K-Lens-M Komments* (August, 1963)

❖ If someone were to pay you ten cents for every kind word you ever spoke about people and collect five cents for every unkind word, would you be rich or poor?

❖ The man deserving a kindness is the fellow who quickly passes it on when it comes to him.

❖ No one is useless in this world who lightens the burden of it to anyone else. – *Dickens*

❖ A smile is a curve that can set a lot of things straight.

❖ If you don't like somebody, you don't need to tell them.

❖ Cultivate enthusiasm. People will like you better for it; you will escape the dull routine of a mechanical existence and you will make headway wherever you are. – *Jonathan Ogden Armour*

❖ The best portion of a good man's life is his little, nameless, unremembered acts of kindness and love.

❖ A polite man today is one who offers a lady his seat when he gets off the bus.

❖ The bigger the heart, the less room there is in it for bitterness.

❖ There is no substitute for a smile. – *K-Lens-M Komments* (October, 1965)

❖ Kindness is one thing you can't give away. It always comes back. – *Sidney Skolsky*

❖ There's no better exercise for strengthening the heart than reaching down and lifting people up. – *Women's Home Companion*

❖ What sunshine is to flowers, smiles are to humanity. Keep some on hand all the time.

❖ You must give up some time to your fellow man. Even if it's a little thing, do something for those who have need of help, something for which you get no pay but the privilege of doing it. For remember, you don't live in a world all your own. Your brothers are here, too. – *Albert Schweitzer*

❖ One good turn and we expect another. – *K-Lens-M Komments* (March, 1964)

❖ He who passes by an opportunity to do good in order to find a better one will search in vain.

❖ 'Tis fine to be a gentleman, but it's a handicap in a good argument.

❖ If you do not have charity in your heart, you have the worst kind of heart trouble.

❖ The kindness we mean to show tomorrow cures no headaches today.

❖ Nothing is ever lost by politeness—except your seat on a bus.

❖ People who address you as "buddy," "chum," "my friend," or "pal," are not being overly friendly. They have merely forgotten your name.

❖ Kind words are short to speak, but their echoes are endless.

❖ When in doubt, do the friendliest thing.

❖ Keep pace with your good intentions and you will be the world's fastest sprinter.

❖ No face is so handsome that a smile can't improve it.

❖ Kindness is one commodity of which we should spend more than we earn. – *K-Lens-M Komments* (July, 1964)

❖ We sometimes wonder if the Golden Rule, too, has been buried at Fort Knox.

❖ People who aim to do good in this life seldom miss the target.

❖ You will never offend a person by returning a smile.

❖ Eventually the man with push overtakes the man with a pull.

❖ If you really intend to make good somewhere, why not start right where you are.

❖ Too much of the milk of human kindness is kept in a frozen state.

❖ A gentleman is one who takes less than he is entitled to take and gives more than he is obliged to give.

❖ Courtesy is contagious. If you don't want to catch it, stay away from it.

❖ Politeness is a virtue, costs little and has great purchasing power. – *Alcott*

❖ Do good and don't look back.

Language

❖ True eloquence consists of saying all that is necessary and nothing more.

❖ You can't add to your stature by multiplying your words.

❖ A joke is a form of humor enjoyed by some and misunderstood by many.

❖ Diary: penned-up emotions. – *Iowa Herald*

❖ We wonder if they still use Latin on tombstones because it is a dead language.

❖ Like a small boy with a knife, a person with a sharp tongue never knows when to stop using it.

❖ Intense: where Boy Scouts sleep. – *John Krivacsy*

❖ The ability to speak in many languages is valuable, but the ability to keep your mouth shut in one is priceless.

❖ Suit of armor: knightgown. – *O. W. Piette*

❖ Some people confuse a moral vocabulary with a good life.

❖ English is compulsory in high school so that students will graduate knowing a language other than their own.

❖ Gargoyle: a spittin' image. – *David A. Schroeder*

❖ Drought: a period during which you can get the dresser drawers open. – *John M. Henry*

❖ Poetry is a way of taking life by the throat. – *Robert Frost*

❖ Profanity is merely a way of escape for a man who runs out of ideas.

❖ It often shows a fine command of language to say nothing. – *The Irish Digest*

❖ Blunt person: one who says what he thinks without thinking. – *Sherrill Penny*

❖ Writers may now discard the use of the exclamation point. People are not surprised at anything these days.

❖ Bookie: wizard of odds. – *Arthur Wellikoff*

❖ An autobiography usually reveals nothing bad about its writer except his memory. – *Franklin P. Jones*

Surprising Facts by K-Lens-M Komments

✓ There are about 700,000 words in the dictionary. (August, 1964)
✓ There are nearly a thousand languages in Africa alone. (October, 1965)

English As She Is

We'll begin with a box and the plural is boxes,
But the plural of ox should be oxen not oxes.
The one fowl is a goose but two are called geese,
Yet the plural of mouse should never be meese.
If the plural of man is always called men,
Why shouldn't the plural of pan be called pen?
If I speak of a foot and you show me your feet,
And I give you a boot would a pair be called beet?
We speak of a brother and also of brethren,
But though we say mother we never say methren.
Then the masculine pronouns are he, him, and his,
But imagine the feminine she, shim and shis.
So English I fancy you all will agree,
It's the funniest language you ever did see.

Life In General

❖ Horse sense, quite naturally, will be found dwelling in a stable mind.

❖ Collisions are bound to occur when great minds run in the same channel.

❖ If all men were born free, it's time the hospitals were told about it.

❖ Adversity is the most thorough teacher in the school of experience.

❖ Ideas are very much like children—your own are wonderful.

❖ Don't grumble because roses have thorns. Let's be thankful that thorny bushes have roses.

❖ Life is a continuous cycle of getting and giving, and forgetting and forgiving.

❖ The trouble with slacks is that we seldom see a pair that is slack enough.

❖ A birth certificate is sometimes a lie detector.

❖ Sometimes it costs dearly to get rid of things you get for nothing.

❖ The college yell in the school of experience is silence.

❖ A flood is just a river that is too big for its bridges.

❖ Maybe the ocean roars because so many bathers step on its tow.

❖ Excuses seldom serve the purpose for which they were intended.

❖ The things that make life worth living are always the things people have.

❖ People who are not thankful for what they receive should be thankful for what they escape.

❖ Half of life is giving in—the other half is giving out.
  – *K-Lens-M Komments* (October, 1965)

❖ The future has a way of repaying those who are patient with it.
  – *The Reverend Arthur Pringle*

❖ Nothing widens a narrow driveway quite as much as looking at it with a snow shovel in your hands. – *David O. Flynn*

❖ It has always seemed to be a rule of life that you receive many more complaints than compliments.

❖ It takes more than hot air to keep breezing along. – *K-Lens-M Komments* (August, 1964)

❖ The road to ruin is well lighted, and the traffic lights are always green.

❖ Sleeping bag: a nap sack. – *Bob Dreitzer*

❖ Strange as it may seem, the heavy end of a match is its light end.

❖ The cost of safety goes up when you try to get along without it.

❖ It seems to be human nature for the man who is asked to take a back seat to take affront.

❖ An alarm clock is a device that scares the sleep out of you.

❖ "Beautiful snow" depends a lot on whether you have a shovel or not. – *Mrs. C. L. Archibald*

❖ Gracious living is when you have the house air conditioned, and then load the yard with chairs, lounges and an outdoor oven so you can spend all your time in the hot sun. – *Detroit News*

❖ To live and learn may be all right, but by the time some people learn it is too late to live.

❖ The best things may not always be best for us. – *K-Lens-M Komments* (May, 1965)

❖ Gift shop: a place where you can see all the things you hope your friends won't send you for Christmas. – *Jack Woolsey in Point*

❖ Life can only be understood backward, but it must be lived forward. – *Sören Kierkegaard*

❖ The difference between the North Pole and the South Pole is all the difference in the world.

❖ What usually makes them "good old days" is a rich imagination and a poor memory.

❖ Nothing is more restful than a warm, crackling fire in the living room—if you have a fireplace.

❖ He who masters a hard life accomplishes much more than he who is mastered by an easy one.

❖ Life is a grindstone: whether it grinds you down or polishes you up depends on what you're made of. – *Anonymous*

❖ One trouble with this country is the number of people trying to get something for nothing. Another trouble is the high percentage of those who succeed.

❖ Impossible is an excuse the world no longer accepts. – *K-Lens-M Komments* (July, 1964)

❖ It is just as important to know your way out as to know your way in.

❖ Life may be short, but that is no reason for you to believe that your good resolution will outlive you.

❖ The catastrophe threatening to crush us in one fell swoop harms us less than our own indolence or indecision. – *K-Lens-M Komments* (August, 1963)

❖ Man's interference with nature's plans nearly always brings a disastrous reaction.

❖ For some of us, roughing it means turning the electric blanket down to medium.

❖ Life is that interval between the time your teeth are almost through and the time you are through with your teeth.

❖ "Mine" and "Thine" are the sources of all lawsuits.

❖ Life is a taxi; the meter keeps on going whether you are getting somewhere or just sitting still.

❖ Most of us would appreciate the beautiful morning more if it didn't come so early in the day.

❖ The real problem in life is not so much where we stand, but what we stand for.

❖ Flattery is something nice someone tells you that you wish to heaven were true.

❖ Perfect timing: being able to turn off the "hot" and "cold" shower faucets at the same time. – *Karen Chandler*

❖ In a beauty shop: "Sale of wigs—six months toupee." – *Hugh Allen*

❖ Another thing that loses its grip as it grows older is an old suitcase.

❖ We never seem to know what anything means until we have lost it.

❖ Hypocrites set good examples only when there is an audience.

❖ Honest folks who ask for only what's right, usually get left.

❖ No matter how hard you try, you won't leave this world alive.

❖ The easiest thing in the world is to go from bad to worse.

❖ The early bird not only gets the worm, but gets the first whack at the morning newspaper.

❖ It is impossible to find any rule of conduct to excel simplicity and sincerity.

❖ Life may be short, yet it gives most men time to outlive their good intentions.

❖ A small town is a place where everybody knows what everybody else is doing, but they read the local paper to see if they've been caught at it.

❖ Life is what we make it and how we take it. – *K–Lens–M Komments* (July, 1964)

❖ The bitterness of poor quality lingers long after the sweetness of the price is forgotten.

❖ Enough: more than you have. – *K–Lens–M Komments* (August, 1963)

❖ Take good care of the present and trade it in on a better future.

❖ Millions of people are dissatisfied with the world, but few are trying to do anything about it.

❖ Ointment is stuff that when something goes wrong there is a fly in it.

❖ To go slowly and to live a long time are two brothers.

❖ The trouble with letting well enough alone is in knowing when anything *is* well enough. — *Nuggets*

❖ On a certain island in the South Pacific there are no taxes, unemployment, crime, beggars, jazz bands, TV or inhabitants. – *The Expanding Circle*

❖ Men are rewarded for what they give the world—not what they take.

❖ Farm: what a city-man dreams of at 5 p.m., never at 5 a.m. – *Joseph Marturano*

❖ Trouble is more often caused by the things we let slip through our lips rather than those which slip through our fingers.

❖ The largest room in the world is room for improvement.

❖ The world seems cold-hearted only to the man who tries to live on its generosity.

❖ Wood: that remarkable material which burns so easily in a forest and with such difficulty in the fireplace. – *Bill Vaughan*

❖ The last thing we learn is to put first things first. – *K-Lens-M Komments* (July, 1964)

❖ A lot of homes have been spoiled by inferior desecrators. – *Frank Lloyd Wright*

❖ A better day is coming if you can distinguish it when it arrives.

❖ Saving the world would be much easier than to try to convince it that it is lost.

❖ The scheme of life seems to be that the good die young, and the older we grow, the more chance we have of being found out.

❖ It's easy to laugh at misfortunes if you are the one they miss.

❖ We're seldom aware of what's cooking until it boils over.

❖ Life is ten percent what you make it, and ninety percent how you take it.

❖ Whether health or wealth is the greater blessing depends on which you have.

❖ The measure of any kind of trouble depends a lot on whether it is coming or going.

❖ He who buys what he doesn't need steals from himself.

❖ Life is an everlasting struggle to keep money coming in and teeth and hair from coming out.

❖ It's not the distance but the direction you travel that counts.

❖ The cold still grips the garden plot, the snow lies in every spot, but still the crocus knows it not. – *Barbara A. Jones*

❖ Junk: something you keep ten years and then throw away two weeks before you need it. – *Gloria Ray*

❖ A good part of our lives is spent in getting used to the things we didn't expect.

❖ Some people spend half their time complaining about the shortness of life's span, and the other half killing time.

❖ In the game of life, the man to watch the closest is yourself.

❖ Good resolutions always increase in value by setting good examples for others to follow.

❖ Nothing makes a lumpy mattress more comfortable than the ringing of an alarm clock.

❖ Be a good bookkeeper in the game of life. A good bookkeeper can't afford to lose his balance.

❖ Civilization is a system under which a man pays a half dollar to park his car so he won't be fined two dollars while spending a dime for a nickel cup of coffee.

❖ The eighth wonder of the world is wondering what will happen next.

❖ Flashlight: a case in which to carry dead batteries.
  – *David H. Robbins*

❖ When worse comes to worse, people find it best to make the best of it.

❖ A straight tip on a sure thing usually demonstrates the uncertainties of life.

❖ Recipe for a long life: be moderate in all things, but don't miss anything.

❖ Most of the footprints on the sands of time were left there by work shoes.

❖ The Golden Rule is of no use whatever unless you realize it's your move. – *Leo Aikman*

❖ The school of experience really makes it tough for the chap who tries to cut classes.

❖ Some books have happy endings; others are loaned.

❖ Do not fear your motives being misunderstood or not understood at all. Fear far more for them to be understood in their entirety.
  – *Franz Marchault*

❖ The first signs of spring are those warning that the highway is under construction. – *Harold Coffin*

❖ Circumstances are neutral. All depends on what we do with them.

❖ When the grass looks greener on the other side of the fence, it may be that they take better care of it there.

❖ If you keep looking back, you may go that way.

❖ Fall is the season when you find out which won—the moth or the mothballs.

❖ Only people who have nothing to do look upon life as a burden.

❖ Coiffure: French word meaning, "You'll keep coming back to us because you'll never be able to do it this way yourself." – *"Fibber McGee and Molly"*

❖ You are never in worse company than when you fly into a rage and are beside yourself.

❖ Next to Christmas and payday, the most anticipated thing is a green traffic light.

❖ New homes come equipped with every modern convenience except low monthly payments and low taxes, and everything in them is controlled by switches except the children.

❖ It is change, not love, that makes the world go round; love only keeps it populated. – *Charles H. Brower*

❖ A free ride is usually on the wrong road.

❖ One always tends to overpraise a long book because one has got through it. – *E. M. Forster*

❖ Fall by the wayside in the race of life and you won't even get paid for the mileage you've run.

❖ There are two ways of spreading light: to be the candle, or the mirror that reflects it. – *Edith Wharton, quoted in Robins Reader*

Life In General

❖ Rules are for when brains run out. – *George Papashvily*

❖ Mummies are Egyptians that were pressed for time.
   – *Ralph Mitchell*

❖ Life hardens what is soft within us and softens what is hard.
   – *Dr. Joseph Fort Newton*

❖ Most of the trouble people get into these days is through their
   mouths—either eating, drinking or talking.

❖ Take life as you find it, but don't leave it that way.

❖ Just about the only thing a nickel is good for these days is to get
   the wrong number on a telephone.

❖ What this country needs is not a good five-cent cigar, or a good
   five-cent cup of coffee, but a good five cents.
   – *The Rosary Magazine*

❖ No use borrowing trouble—there are always people willing to
   give it to you.

❖ Progress is the development of more machinery to provide more
   people with more leisure in which to be bored.

❖ Life is our friend. It wasn't meant to be anyone's enemy.

❖ No labor saving device in the world can beat a wastebasket.

❖ It is difficult to say what is impossible, for the dream of yesterday
   is the hope of today and the reality of tomorrow.
   – *Robert Goddard*

❖ Life lived just to satisfy yourself usually satisfies no one.

❖ Everything is much simpler today. Instead of solving a problem, you just subsidize it. – *Bill Vaughan*

❖ Life teaches us one serious lesson: you must be a comer or you're a goner.

❖ Experience is not what happens to you; it is what you do with what happens to you. – *Aldous Huxley*

❖ The difference between a fiddle and a violin depends on who is playing it.

❖ Some people's only ambition in life is to continue breathing.

❖ Spring is when the days become longer and the underwear shorter.

❖ Sometimes we think the world is growing worse, but it may just be that the news and radio coverage are better. – *Anonymous*

❖ A bargain is something you have to find use for once you've bought it. – *Franklin P. Jones*

❖ Among life's most embarrassing moments are those spent in re-crossing the stream after the bridges have been burned.

❖ Life is an ill-spent legacy. – *K-Lens-M Komments* (October, 1963)

❖ If you know your business, you'll never have to explain to others the reasons for what you do.

❖ A hick town is one where there is no place to go that you shouldn't.

❖ The reason history repeats itself is that most people weren't listening the first time. – *Dan Bennett*

❖ Many people lose an argument with an alarm clock because they take it lying down.

❖ Some people get up bright and early; some of us just get up early; while some just get up.

❖ A well-ordered life is like climbing a tower; the view halfway up is better than the view from the base, and it steadily becomes finer as the horizon expands.
– *William Lyon Phelps, Autobiography (Oxford)*

❖ Getting to a cocktail party late is like trying to get on a merry-go-round after it has started. – *Dan Bennett*

❖ Sleep is a condition in which some people talk, some work, some snore.

❖ One way to keep them down on the farm is to pay them for not planting a crop. – *Carey Williams*

❖ You can't always judge by appearances. The early bird may have been up all night.

❖ He who is let in on the ground floor usually finds there is no roof over it.

❖ There is not much difference between living and dying; each one has to do it for himself.

❖ The world changes so fast that a man couldn't be wrong all the time if he tried.

❖ Those who think the world is against them are traveling on the right road to make it so.

❖ Cyclones aren't the only twisters. – *K-Lens-M Komments* (August, 1965)

❖ The greatest use of life is to spend it for something that will outlive it.

❖ Nothing modernizes a home so completely as an ad offering it for sale. – *Franklin P. Jones*

❖ Boredom is an emptiness filled with insistence. – *Leo Stein*

❖ The impossible is something no one can do until someone goes ahead and does it.

❖ If the worst is yet to come, why worry now?

❖ By the time a man can afford a shampoo in a barbershop, he hasn't any hair left.

❖ Home is where the mortgage is. – *K-Lens-M Komments* (April, 1964)

❖ Once a man starts down hill, so-called friends are always ready to push.

❖ Those who complain about the way the ball bounces are often the ones who dropped it.

❖ The improbable happens just often enough to make life either disturbing or delightful. – *William Feather*

❖ The fellow who laughs last may laugh best, but he gets the reputation of being a dumbbell.

❖ The dividing line between right and wrong seems to be invisible to some people.

❖ A man's life is dyed the color of his imagination.
  – *Marcus Aurelius*

❖ Some strapless gowns may not be nice, but not as shocking as the price. – *K-Lens-M Komments* (October, 1963)

❖ One of the exasperating things about inflation is that, even though the price of haircuts keeps going up, they don't last any longer. – *The Wall Street Journal*

❖ Winter is like long underwear—it creeps up on you. – *K-Lens-M Komments*

❖ You can't start a new life without first discarding the old.

❖ How satisfying it is to park on the time left by the other fellow's nickel.

❖ It pays to remember that all of our yesterdays were todays and all of our todays were once tomorrows.

❖ Every time history repeats itself the price goes up.

❖ We may complain about heat in the summer, but at least we don't have to shovel it.

❖ Nothing makes a new dress such a pleasing success, as to see it for more in a different store. – *May Richstone*

❖ We wonder why luck changes so much quicker when it's good.
  – *K-Lens-M Komments*

❖ The scales of justice seem off balance when the time comes for us to face the judge.

❖ If it were just as easy to arouse enthusiasm as it is suspicion, think what good could be accomplished.

❖ The world is not interested in the storms you encountered, but did you bring in the ship?

❖ We never seem to know what anything means until we have lost it.

❖ Footnotes: dance music. – *K-Lens-M Komments*

❖ Considering the price of haircuts today, two heads are not better than one.

❖ If it weren't for modern home appliances, you'd never have time to keep them in repair. – *Franklin P. Jones*

❖ We all want to get the news objectively, impartially and from our own point of view. – *Bill Vaughan*

❖ Affliction, as does the blacksmith, shapes as it smites.

❖ The glass that cheers isn't a full-length mirror. – *K-Lens-M Komments* (May, 1964)

❖ The higher the price of a haircut, the longer the hair grows between cuts.

❖ Life has two ends and one of them has been used; better take care of the other one.

❖ It is impossible to cheat life. There are no answers to the problems of life in the back of the book. – *Sören Kierkegaard*

❖ Autumn, a second spring when every leaf is a flower. – *Albert Camus*

❖ Spring cleaning: rearranging dust. – *K-Lens-M Komments*

❖ The trouble with our times is that the future is not what it used to be. – *Paul Valéry*

❖ We can't cross a bridge until we come to it; but I always like to lay down a pontoon ahead of time. – *Bernard Baruch*

❖ Swimming pool: a small body of water completely surrounded by neighbors. – *K-Lens-M Komments* (September, 1963)

❖ Four things come not back: the spoken word; the sped arrow; time past; the neglected opportunity—the saying of the second caliph.

❖ A fashion ten years before its time is indecent. Ten years after its time it is hideous. After a century it becomes romantic. – *James Laver*

❖ We feel sorry for the man who wants to live in the country. He has moved out of town three times and each time the city overtook him.

❖ Some things have to be believed to be seen. – *Ralph Hodgson*

❖ Much of the good work of the world has been that of dull people who have done their best. – *Senator George F. Hoar*

❖ There may not be much to be seen in a small town, but what you hear will more than make up for it.

❖ You can't make your mark with an eraser. – *K-Lens-M Komments* (September, 1963)

❖ Nearly all the best sellers in modern fiction are divisible into types—neurotic, erotic and tommyrot.

❖ Grass may grow greener on the other side of the fence, but it needs mowing oftener on this side. – *R. J. Jensen*

❖ Rain: eavesdropper. – *K-Lens-M Komments*

❖ Seeing is not always believing. Many people we see cannot be believed.

❖ Many of the newest hairdos look not quite done. – *Indianapolis News*

❖ Cultivation of good habits helps to weed out the bad ones.

❖ There are fewer shipwrecks now, but many are wrecks before they board. – *K-Lens-M Komments* (July, 1964)

❖ There are in nature neither rewards nor punishments. There are consequences. – *R. G. Ingersoll*

❖ Most people like different seasons. In summer they like winter, and in winter they like summer.

❖ Why do they call it idle curiosity when it's working all the time? – *K-Lens-M Komments*

❖ Resolutions to reform come from those who have been detected.

❖ One thing about the speed of light—it gets here too soon in the morning. – *The Wall Street Journal*

❖ If you can't find it in the dictionary, ask for it at the drug store.

❖ Life isn't all you crack up to be. – *K-Lens-M Komments*

❖ Perhaps the reason so many accidents happen in the home is that some people don't spend enough time there to learn their way around.

❖ Consciousness in a small town is ably assisted by the neighbors.

❖ An American is a guy who will spend half a day looking for pills to make him live longer, then drive 90 miles an hour to make up the time he has lost.

❖ Every dogma has its day. – *K-Lens-M Komments* (April, 1964)

❖ People who live in glass houses have to answer the bell. – *The Pointer*

❖ The tragedy of life is not so much what men suffer, but rather what they miss. – *Thomas Carlyle*

❖ Iftheworldpopulationexplosioncontinuespeoplewillbepackedas- closeasthis. – *K-Lens-M Komments* (March, 1964)

❖ The nicest thing about the promise of spring is that sooner or later she'll have to keep it. – *Mark Beltaire*

❖ The minute a man goes down, his enemies quit kicking him and his friends begin.

❖ Foresight: resting before you get tired. – *K-Lens-M Komments* (May, 1963)

❖ Don't worry about your station in life; somebody will be sure to tell you where to get off.

❖ Days are getting shorter and so are we. – *K-Lens-M Komments* (October, 1963)

❖ First a howling blizzard woke us, then the rain came down to soak us, and now before the eye can focus—crocus. – *Lilja Rogers*

❖ When a reader complains that the news in a publication is slanted, his complaint is that the slant is not in the direction of his prejudices.

❖ Home: the only place you can trust hash … or a compliment.
– *K-Lens-M Komments* (July, 1964)

❖ Napoleon is reported to have once said he feared his allies more than his enemies.

❖ To live remains an art which everyone can learn, and which no one can teach.

❖ If you keep going nowhere, that is where you'll get.
– *K-Lens-M Komments* (April, 1964)

❖ Many people are on the way, but few have a definite idea where they want to go.

❖ Falling hair may cause despair, but few object to falling heir.
– *K-Lens-M Komments*

❖ A secret is something that you tell only one person at a time.

❖ A small town is where everyone knows whose check is good and whose husband isn't.

❖ History is the sum total of the things that could have been avoided. – *Konrad Adenauer*

❖ We owe to the Middle Ages the two worst inventions of humanity—romantic love and gunpowder. – *André Maurois*

❖ Variety is the spice of life but monotony provides the groceries.

❖ Shoplifting: free enterprise. – *K-Lens-M Komments*

❖ With such a wide, wide world, it's a mystery why some people live on such a narrow margin.

Surprising Facts by K-Lens-M Komments

- ✓ It takes a minimum of 15 gallons of water for a tub bath—about three gallons per minute for a shower. (June, 1962)
- ✓ There are fewer colorblind women than men. (October, 1963)
- ✓ Varying the color of objects changes their apparent distance. (October, 1963)
- ✓ Red, yellow, and blue are the three primary colors. (October, 1963)
- ✓ Color is a property of light. (October, 1963)
- ✓ Taupe is yellowish. (October, 1963)
- ✓ Mauve is purplish. (October, 1963)
- ✓ About 28,000,000 Americans move every year. (April, 1964)
- ✓ Some orchid seeds are 35,000,000 to the ounce (if you don't believe it count 'em) (July, 1964)
- ✓ New York City has three times as many automobiles as France and Germany combined. (August, 1964)

Love

❖ This may be a man's world, but women are partly to blame for the shape it's in.

❖ No matter how poor a man may be, he is usually willing to share his poverty with a woman.

❖ We like someone *because*. We love someone *although*.
  – *Henri de Montherlant*

❖ Cosmetics are a woman's way of keeping men from reading between the lines.

❖ Quite frequently, a girl gets rid of a headache by telling him she has one.

❖ When a fellow gets married, his spooning days are over; from then on, he has to fork it over.

❖ Husband-hunting is probably the only sport in which the animal that gets caught has to buy a license.

❖ Marriage is the best incubator of maturity. – *K-Lens-M Komments* (October, 1965)

❖ How strange it is that when a man does not have a worry in the world, he gets married.

❖ The fellow who married a church choir singer said they met by chants.

❖ A man who thinks marriage is a 50-50 proposition doesn't understand one of two things—women or fractions.

❖ An unhappy gal is Sally Snide; never a bridesmaid—always a bride. – *K-Lens-M Komments* (June, 1962)

❖ A gentleman is one who, when his wife drops something, kicks it over to her so she can pick it up.

❖ A local young man told a pretty girl that she looked like a million dollars. She replied, "Thanks, and I'm just as hard to make."

❖ Some men marry because they are hopeful; some because they are curious. Frequently both are disappointed.

❖ The clinging gowns a husband cheers are those his wife clings to for years. – *K-Lens-M Komments* (June, 1962)

❖ Some husbands have lost their liberty in the pursuit of happiness.

❖ An old-timer is one who can remember when a dishwashing machine had to be married, not bought.

❖ A honeymoon is a sort of vacation a man takes before going to work for a new boss.

❖ Nothing prepares a man for marriage as much as a girl. – *Homer Phillips*

❖ Frequently when a girl marries she gives up the attention of several men for the inattention of one.

❖ Don't marry for better or worse—marry for good. – *K-Lens-M Komments* (May, 1963)

❖ Going to a party with your wife is like going on a hunting trip with a game warden.

- ❖ Love is just a chemical reaction. But it's fun trying to find the formula. – *J. D. Shantel*

- ❖ Some girls, while waiting for the right man to come along, have wonderful times with the wrong ones.

- ❖ Flattery gets a gal nowhere—but to the altar. – *K-Lens-M Komments* (June, 1962)

- ❖ A woman has no right to question the love of a husband who is willing to wear the neckties she buys for him.

- ❖ The model husband is the one who turns over a new leaf for his wife—in his checkbook.

- ❖ The male half of a particularly happy couple claims that the wife who always cooks her husband's favorite dishes will always be his favorite dish.

- ❖ Occasionally a man can pull the wool over his wife's eyes with the wrong yarn.

- ❖ Bad luck never comes singly; sometimes it comes married.

- ❖ If a man wants a wife who can cook and sew and neither smokes nor drinks, he should go to the graveyard and dig one up.

- ❖ There's nothing like a heavenly body to make a man stare into space. – *Cy N. Peace*

- ❖ Someone has said that a wedding is a funeral at which you can smell your own flowers.

- ❖ Some of the hottest arguments between husband and wife are cooked up over an old flame.

❖ A man can usually tell what kind of a time he is having at a party by the look on his wife's face.

❖ Life is just one full thing after another. Love is just two fool things after each other.

❖ The University of Tennessee's student newspaper column of engagements and marriages is titled: "Who's Whose"
 – *Oliver Towne in St. Paul Dispatch*

❖ A girl doesn't have to be very muscular to pick up a man.

❖ A neighbor tells us that his wife talks to herself, but doesn't realize it—she thinks he is listening.

❖ Puppy love is sometimes the beginning of a dog's life.

❖ Wonder if they throw shoes at brides and bridegrooms because they got married on a shoestring.

❖ To most female teenagers, a thing of beauty is a boy forever.
 – *Demaris Moody*

❖ When a man breaks a date he usually has to. When a girl breaks a date she usually has two.

❖ An extravagance is anything you buy that is of no earthly use to your wife. – *Franklin P. Jones*

❖ Sometimes a woman doesn't seem to care for a man's company unless he owns it.

❖ Said one elderly gentleman to another, "Every time I stay late at the club my wife thinks I'm out chasing women. Gad! I wish she were right."

❖ A woman who reads her husband like a book has to be clever to avoid wearing out the binding.

❖ Tell a girl she is pretty and she will like it, but will not be sure you are in earnest; tell her she is prettier than some girl she knows is pretty and you have got her. – *Anonymous*

❖ Said one younger nurse to another: "I've been eating an apple a day for weeks, but that new doctor still chases me."

❖ A wolf is a fellow who wants his hands on a girl, but who doesn't want a girl on his hands.

❖ When a woman loves a man, he can make her do anything she wants to.

❖ Absence may make the heart grow fonder, but presents make for better results!

❖ A sweet young bride said, "I didn't want to marry Bill for his money. It's just that there was no other way to get it."

❖ Women think about love more than men, that's because men think more about women. – *Quote in Les Nouvelles Littéraires*

❖ Nothing is so gratifying to a wife than to see a double chin on her husband's old flame.

❖ As soon as you cannot keep anything from a woman, you love her. – *Paul Géraldy*

❖ Isn't it amazing the way nature can produce a beautiful diamond

merely by taking a man and putting him under terrific pressure?
– *The Hub*

❖ "When we were first married we got along fine, but as we were leaving the church . . . ."

❖ A few girls prefer to remain single, but the majority would rather knot.

❖ Don't be too critical of your wife's judgment. Remember, it was her decision to marry you.

❖ A bachelor has been described as a selfish man who has cheated some worthy woman out of a divorce.

❖ You can't always tell what makes a man tick until you meet his wife. She may be the works. – *Franklin P. Jones*

❖ A fellow who burns the candle at both ends may have two flames. – *Cy N. Peace*

❖ It's difficult to understand why the wife never asks the husband if he locked all the doors until he's snug in bed.

❖ Some men quarrel with their wives and others have learned to say, "Yes, dear."

❖ Every woman needs five husbands—an intellectual companion, a muscular toiler, a financial genius, a romantic playboy, and a practical plumber.

❖ Marriage ties: kind wives buy. – *K-Lens-M Komments* (March, 1964)

❖ Every man needs five wives—a movie sweetheart, an English valet, a hotel chef, an attentive audience, and a trained nurse.

❖ The other half lives exactly the way their better half lets them.

❖ Marriage vows are none too strong—for better or worse, but not for long. – *K-Lens-M Komments* (March, 1964)

❖ The best way to keep from getting cold feet at a wedding is to hot-foot it out of town.

❖ The magician who saws a woman in two isn't nearly as marvelous as the husband who keeps one from flying to pieces.
– *Nat Curran*

❖ Engagement: to ring a belle. – *K-Lens-M Komments* (March, 1964)

❖ Wife to husband: "All right, we'll compromise. Admit you're wrong, and I'll forgive you." – *Bob Barnes*

❖ Rules are the only means of a girl's assessing which man she likes well enough to break them for. – *Petronella Portobello*

❖ To most modern writers, sex is a novel idea. – *Playboy*

❖ A diamond — a stepping stone in every girl's life.

❖ Now is when true love doesn't run smooth—it stops and parks.
– *Sid Ascher*

❖ A suitor rarely can support a girl in the style to which he accustoms her.

❖ We used to hear so much about youngsters running away from the home to get married. In this day and time, they get married and run back home.

❖ It's better to have loved and lost than to have to do the homework for six kids.

Love

❖ Men are attracted by a fire and women by the sale that follows.

❖ No girl is ever insulted by a proposition that has a genuine ring to it. – *Dan Bennett*

❖ The husband who says he's never looked at another woman must be discouraged. – *K-Lens-M Komments*

❖ Wedded bliss: we suppose you would call a wedding ring a one-man band. – *The Re-Saw*

❖ Most girls list as life's chief blisses: being missed and being Mrs. – *Stephen Schlitzer*

❖ A man never knows that a woman has any old clothes until he marries her. – *Derek Wingrave*

❖ When a man changes his mind as much as a woman, chances are he's married to her.

❖ He was a gay dog, but now he's spouse-broken. – *Norfolk Virginian-Pilot*

❖ The bonds of matrimony are like any other bonds—they take a while to mature. – *Peter De Vries*

❖ A practical nurse is one who marries a wealthy patient.

❖ It is also possible that blondes prefer gentlemen. – *Town Journal*

❖ Some people can remember when no lipsticks were kiss-proof, but most girls were.

❖ The woman who arranges a match for her daughter often expects to referee it, too.

❖ Many a sleepless gal suffers from Himsomnia. – *K-Lens-M Komments*

❖ Girls are always running through his mind—they don't dare walk. – *Mike Connolly*

❖ A bachelor is a man with no ties, except those that need cleaning.

❖ Lieutenant commander: a lieutenant's wife. – *Calgary Albertan*

❖ After all is said and done, it's usually the wife who has said it and the husband who has done it. – *Sammy Kaye*

❖ Just give the average young man two tickets to a football game, the nice fresh air, and a beautiful girl to take to the game, and you can keep the two tickets and the nice fresh air. – *Earl Wilson*

❖ A neighbor's wife said, "John and I like the same things—but it took him twelve years to learn."

❖ "If you refuse me," swore a young swain, "I shall die." She refused him. Sixty-three years later, he died.

❖ Leisure: the two minutes' rest a man gets while his wife thinks up something for him to do. – *Enterprise*

❖ Gals loved for their minds get kissed on the forehead. – *K-Lens-M Komments*

❖ A missile can't take you out of this world like a kiss'll.

❖ Marriages frequently go on the rocks because a girl married a night owl and expected him to become a homing pigeon.

❖ The honeymoon is over when the wife complains about the noise her husband makes while preparing his own breakfast.

❖ Hash and romance are best enjoyed when the customer doesn't give too much thought to what's in 'em.

❖ Any old hen looks like a chicken to a man who is starving for food or love.

❖ Her wallop gave him quite a jar—he changed gears in a compact car. – *K-Lens-M Komments*

❖ Bachelor: a guy who wouldn't change his quarters for a better half.

❖ Bachelor: a man who leans toward women, but not far enough to altar his stance. – *Al Spong*

❖ Bachelor: a man who'd rather have a woman on his mind than on his neck. – *Charles Guy*

❖ Many a woman has started out playing with fire and ended up cooking over one.

❖ Bachelor: a man who never Mrs. anybody.

❖ He has decided opinions—his wife decides them for him. – *Vindicator*

❖ Marriage: when a man gets hooked with his own line. – *Automotive Dealer News*

❖ There's always one girl at every dance who makes the others wish they'd gone to the movies. – *Irving Hoffman*

❖ Thee subjects that give college men the most trouble live in sorority houses.

❖ In the matrimonial sweepstakes, the diamond means that the young lady is, or should be, on her last lap. – *Frank L. Murphy*

❖ Don't expect the wolves to howl if you slap on makeup with a trowel. – *K-Lens-M Komments*

❖ Split affinities: she took him for better or worse but he was worse than she took him for. – *Erskine Johnson*

❖ A little yearning, now and then, is cherished by the best of men.

❖ Blind date: when you expect to meet a vision and she turns out to be a sight. – *Southern Pharmaceutical Journal*

❖ We have read of so many people saying definitely they will never marry, but we notice that the building of larger schoolhouses goes on just the same.

❖ Fishermen catch the most in the early morn or just after dark or when they get home. – *Hal Cochran*

❖ Many a girl marries a man and discovers he was telling the truth when he said he wasn't good enough for her.

❖ What's so remarkable about those millionth of a second computers? Smart dames get your number faster than that! – *K-Lens-M Komments*

❖ Honeymoon: a short period of doting between dating and debting. – *Ray C. Bandy*

❖ Flirting: wishful winking. – *Sid Caesar*

❖ If a man's wife consistently makes very poor coffee, would it be grounds for divorce?

❖ There is nothing harder than a diamond except paying for it.

❖ A husband is really broken in when he can understand every word his wife isn't saying. – *Shannon Fife*

❖ In Hollywood, marriage is a rest period between romances.

❖ One way for the husband to get the last word is to apologize. – *Peggy Caroline Fears in The Saturday Evening Post*

❖ One way a girl can stop a man from making love to her is to marry him.

❖ By the time he whispers, "We were made for each other," she's already planning alterations. – *Ivern Boyett*

❖ Never tell a woman you are unworthy of her. Let it come to her as a surprise.

❖ He who has love in his heart has spurs in his heels.

❖ True love runs smoother than the detours. – *K-Lens-M Komments*

❖ Sometimes the law of gravity doesn't work; for instance, it's easier to pick up a girl than it is to drop her. – *Earl Wilson*

❖ The smart man lets his wife have her own way, and most of his.

❖ Hollywood marriage: much "I do" about nothing.

❖ In marriage, it's not as important to pick the right person as it is to *be* the right partner. – *Dr. Paul Popenoe*

❖ Blind love doesn't stay that way. – *K-Lens-M Komments*
(August, 1964)

❖ Bachelor: someone who takes a nap without turning down the bedspread. – *Margaret Pointer*

❖ A woman does not mind seeing her husband make a fool of himself as long as some other woman is not helping him.

❖ You can't kiss a girl unexpectedly. The nearest you can come to it is to kiss her sooner than she thought you would.

❖ She lights his pipe and smokes it, too! – *K-Lens-M Komments*
(May, 1964)

❖ Some girls marry a man because he reminds them of their dad. This may be why mothers cry at weddings.

❖ When a wife really wants something from her husband, getting it takes only a little wile. – *Vesta M. Kelly*

❖ A good wife can do almost anything for a man except put his hat on just right.

❖ All marriages are happy. It's the living together that causes the trouble.

❖ A quick and easy cure for claustrophobia is to be cooped up in a parked car with a pretty girl. – *K-Lens-M Komments*

❖ There are many times when a man wishes he were as smart as his wife's first husband.

❖ Of all the skills a girl should know, the first is how to knot a beau. – *Vesta N. Fairbairn*

Love

❖ They tried to kiss at eighty per; no more him and no more her.

❖ The successful outcome of marriage depends upon the income.

❖ Engagement: verge of a merge. – *K-Lens-M Komments*
(September, 1963)

❖ The only thing some women know about cooking is how to bring their husbands to a boil.

❖ Honeymoon: coo-existence. – *Town Journal*

❖ To the average girl, courtship is the art of not showing her hand until you ask for it. – *Franklin P. Jones*

❖ Diamonds may be highly vaunted but they make a gal feel wanted. – *K-Lens-M Komments* (August, 1964)

❖ Buried treasure is the first husband a woman is always bragging about to the second.

❖ A man's wife may not be the one woman he ever loved, but she's the only one who made him prove it!

❖ Gals who close their eyes when kissing substitute the guy who's missing. – *K-Lens-M Komments* (August, 1964)

❖ If you plan to get married, try to arrange the date so your silver anniversary doesn't fall on your bowling night.

❖ Bachelor: a guy who can't be miss-led. – *K-Lens-M Komments*
(September, 1963)

❖ If wives really dressed to please their husbands, they'd be wearing last year's clothes. – *Florence Winters*

❖ Adam may have had his troubles, but he never had to listen to

Eve brag about all the other men she could have married.

❖ If a man tells a woman she is beautiful, she will overlook most of his other lies.

❖ The world's greatest optimist is the man who weds his secretary and expects to keep dictating to her. – *K-Lens-M Komments* (August, 1963)

❖ If a kiss speaks volumes, it is seldom a first edition. – *Ohio State Sun-Dial*

❖ An old maid is a yes girl who never had a chance to talk.

❖ Some women say they have their husbands eating out of their hands. That's one way to save washing dishes.

❖ Guys used to serenade gals with a guitar—what fetches 'em now is the horn on a car. – *K-Lens-M Komments* (September, 1963)

❖ Faults are thick where love is thin.

❖ All men make mistakes—husbands just find out about them sooner.

❖ A friend tells me that his wife does bird imitations—she watches him like a hawk.

❖ First it's boy meets girl, then it's man waits for wife. – *NEA*

❖ Marry for spite and you may get more than you want. – *K-Lens-M Komments*

❖ Domestic strife is nothing new. As Sir Edward Coke said four centuries ago, "A man's house is his hassle." – *Fletcher Knebel, Register and Tribune Syndicate*

Love

- The magic of first love is our ignorance that it can never end.
  – Disraeli, quoted in Ladies' Home Journal

- One of the sorrows of divorce is that an alimony check won't teach a young boy how to throw a baseball.

- Tranquilizers are powerful. You can shop all day with your wife and come home giggling. *– K-Lens-M Komments* (August, 1963)

- Alimony is the billing without the cooing.

- Soon after the average man says, "I do," he learns a long list of the things he'd better not do.

- Too many girls think a woman's work is done when she sweeps down the aisle. *– Frances Benson*

- They say the game of love has never been postponed because of darkness.

- You only have to mumble a few words in church to get married, and a few in your sleep to get divorced.

- The best way to win a fight with a woman is with your hat. Grab it and run.

- It is safer to go into marriage billfolded than blindfolded.
  – K-Lens-M Komments (March, 1964)

- A husband has been described as a man who wishes he had as much fun when he is out as his wife thinks he does.

- Love may be blind, but it always manages to find a way.

- A retired husband often is a wife's full-time job. *– Ela Harris*

❖ A woman who won't take you for what you are will sometimes take you for what you have. – *The Bulletin*

❖ Faint praise never won a fair lady. – *K-Lens-M Komments* (May, 1965)

❖ The woman who boasts she can read her husband like a book forgets unwritten chapters.

❖ We recently heard about an absent-minded local man who took his wife to dinner instead of his secretary.

❖ More men than women are colorblind, until a flaming redhead swings by. – *K-Lens-M Komments* (March, 1964)

❖ The high divorce rate indicates that the modern girl can't make up her mind to have a man for a hubby or a hobby.

❖ Single blessedness is that sublime state for which many married persons yearn.

❖ A teenage conception of social security is going steady. – *K-Lens-M Komments* (August, 1963)

❖ Some women have learned how to keep a man at a distance—they marry 'em.

❖ The idea about a man picking a wife is just about as absurd as that of an apple picking a farmer.

❖ It's just as well that faint hearts do not win fair ladies. They wouldn't be able to handle them anyway.

❖ No wonder women think a man has a lot of face. He shaves twenty square miles of his face during his lifetime.

❖ Another way to state it – life is what you mate it. – *K-Lens-M*

Komments (March, 1964)

❖ There isn't a married man who hasn't wished at some time that Adam had died with all his ribs.

❖ A popular girl, not only dated but inundated. – *Edward Artin*

❖ If a girl tells you she never goes out with a perfect stranger, just tell her you're not perfect.

❖ The last thing a woman does by hand is put her finger in a wedding band. – *K-Lens-M Komments* (May, 1965)

❖ Whether a man winds up with a nest egg or a goose egg depends upon the chick he marries.

❖ He's a successful man because he has a wife who tells him what to do and a secretary who does it. – *Orville L. Freeman*

❖ A new groom sweeps clean. – *K-Lens-M Komments* (October, 1963)

❖ Don't marry for money. You can borrow it cheaper.

❖ A woman rushed into the registrar of deeds office, and screamed, "Did you, or did you not, issue me this license to marry Jim Jones?" The registrar replied, "I certainly did." "Well," snapped the woman, "what are you going to do about it? He escaped!"

❖ They got married at an early urge. – *Jerry F. Lauck*

❖ The reason that some young brides do not threaten to go home to mother is because mother is seldom home.

❖ Little things make or break a marriage. – *K-Lens-M Komments* (August, 1963)

❖ Marriage is a deal in which a man gives away half his groceries in order to get the other half cooked. – *John Gwynne*

❖ A life without love, a year without summer.

❖ A husband is a curious creature who buys his football tickets in June and his wife's Christmas present on December 24th.

❖ The last word in an argument is what a wife has. Anything a husband says after that is the beginning of another argument. – *Changing Times, The Kiplinger Magazine*

❖ Casanova: ladybug. – *Leonard L. Levinson*

❖ To give an engagement ring at Christmas is to wrap up two futures with one present.

❖ At the present price of board and bed, fools rush in where wise men fear to wed. – *K-Lens-M Komments* (August, 1965)

❖ Marriage may be made in heaven, but many of them are fought out here on earth.

❖ There are too many one-way streets and two-way marriages. – *K-Lens-M Komments* (August, 1963)

❖ A girl becomes a woman when she stops looking for the ideal man and starts looking for a husband.

❖ A good husband soon learns that his better half is always better than half right.

❖ The word bachelor has been thus defined: a fellow who puts on his socks from the other end.

❖ No sleight of hand is harder than refusing a marriage proposal. – *K-Lens-M Komments* (September, 1963)

❖ Love: the feeling that makes a woman make a man make a fool of himself.

❖ Here's to love—the only fire against which there is no insurance.

❖ Marriage is just another union that defies management.

❖ It's tough for a man to face a crisis after she's been waiting up for several hours.

❖ A guy who tells his gal she's pretty as a picture hasn't seen much modern art. – *K-Lens-M Komments*

❖ The easiest way to get your wife's attention is by looking comfortable. – *Franklin P. Jones*

❖ Up to a certain point a man goes with a woman—after that he's taken.

❖ Man of the Hour: the chap whose wife asked him to wait a minute.

❖ Many a girl strikes oil when she runs her fingers through a man's hair.

❖ Wedding shower: start of a reign. – *K-Lens-M Komments*
(October, 1963)

❖ Man is dust. A woman cries on his shoulder and then he is mud.

❖ All work and no play makes Jack a dull boy and Jill a well-to-do widow. – *Raymond Duncan*

❖ Couples hopeful for a happy marriage will do well to remember that in "wedding" the "we" comes before the "I." – *Robert Brault*

❖ Bussing was a lot more popular when it meant kissing instead of hauling the kids around. – *Bill Vaughan*

❖ They're called bachelor girls because that's what they're after. – *K-Lens-M Komments* (October, 1963)

❖ Chorine complaint: "He's the type who likes to keep in touch—all evening long!" – *Karen Morrow*

❖ Some folks' idea of getting down to bedrock is making love to a girl in a stone quarry.

❖ The word "engagement" has two meanings: in war it's a battle, in courtship it's a surrender. – *General Features Corp*

❖ The old-fashioned woman of today is the one who tries to make one husband last a lifetime.

❖ For sheer artistic shaping power, nothing can compare with the daily, year in, year out, gentle abrasion of the woman who, like a river, keeps flowing with an incessant, soft pressure through her man. – *R. L. Ward*

❖ Love letter: noose paper. – *K-Lens-M Komments* (October, 1963)

❖ All the world loves a lover, until he monopolizes the telephone.

❖ Two heads may be better than one—but not in the same house. – *K-Lens-M Komments* (October, 1963)

❖ The best way to see if the charming woman loves you is to place a stray bit of white cotton on your coat sleeve. If she loves you she will pick it off. – *Arthur Pendenys*

❖ All married men should wear something to indicate they're married, says a woman writer—as if a five-year-old suit and a harried look aren't identification enough! – *Grit*

❖ Then there was the fellow who married his first wife's sister because he didn't want to break in a new mother-in-law.

❖ Speaking of dames, you don't get a break; they're hard to get or hard to shake. – *K-Lens-M Komments* (August, 1965)

❖ Successful man: one who earns more than his wife can spend. Successful woman: one who finds such a man.

❖ If advertising can be accused of making people live beyond their means, so can matrimony.

❖ Never marry a contortionist, gals, unless he promises to go straight. – *K-Lens-M Komments* (August, 1965)

❖ Cupid may be a good shot but he sure makes some awful Mrs.

❖ A second look is sometimes the best cure for love at first sight.

❖ Men are such clumsy creatures. They can't slip a ring on a girl's finger without winding up under her thumb.

❖ Chasing girls is great fun if you can find some who will run. – *K-Lens-M Komments* (August, 1963)

❖ Love is like the measles—all the worse when it comes late in life.

❖ Women may be a problem, but they're the kind men like to wrestle with.

❖ Some girls believe the only foundation for true love is a large stone. – *General Futures Corp.*

❖ Love is friendship set to music. – *Pollock*

❖ All is fair in love and peace. – *K-Lens-M Komments* (May, 1963)

❖ Marriage is a committee of two on ways and means. One has her way; the other provides the means.

❖ An ideal husband is what every woman thinks the other woman has.

❖ The gal who lets her I. Q. show takes the twang out of cupid's bow. – *K-Lens-M Komments* (April, 1964)

❖ Quite a number of girls we know are suffering from severe cases of he-fever.

❖ Optimist: a bridegroom who thinks he has no bad habits. – *Hal Chadwick*

❖ Lipstick: red menace women can't keep on and men can't wipe off. – *K-Lens-M Komments* (July, 1964)

❖ Naturally, no one ever gives the groom a shower—he's all washed up anyhow.

❖ Many a man has stopped calling his wife "the little woman" after taking a good look at her in slacks.

❖ Alimony: war debt. – *K-Lens-M Komments* (October, 1963)

❖ Marriage is a process by which the grocer acquires an account the florist had.

❖ The girl who lays all her cards on the table usually ends up by playing solitaire.

❖ A man has only himself to blame for the plainness of his wife; a woman who knows she is loved cannot help but be beautiful. – *Ruth E. Renkel*

❖ Winning at love or war doesn't seem to stop the expenses.
  – *K-Lens-M Komments* (October, 1963)

❖ Bachelor: the only species of big game for which the license is taken out after the safari.

❖ The girl who searches too long for a smart cookie is apt to wind up with a crumb.

Out on a Limerick by Bennett Cert

There was a young man from New York
Whose morals were lighter than cork.
"Young chickens," said he,
"Have no terrors for me:
The bird that *I* fear is the stork!"
— *Hugh Gibson*

There once was a maid in Siam
Who said to her boyfriend, Kiam,
"If you kiss me, of course,
You will have to use force,
But thank goodness you're stronger than I am."
— *Unknown*

There once was a maid with such graces
That her curves cried aloud for embraces.
"You look," said McGee,
"Like a million to me –
Invested in all the right places."
— *Unknown*

Surprising Facts by K-Lens-M Komments

- ✓ 4 out of 10 remarriages fail. (May, 1963)
- ✓ About 93.5 percent of all U.S. girls marry eventually. (July, 1964)

Fidelity & Temptation

- ❖ A man who talks in his sleep may ruin his wife's nerves—if he doesn't speak distinctly.

- ❖ You need not worry about avoiding temptation after you pass fifty. That's when it starts avoiding you.

- ❖ The average number of times a man says "No" to temptation is once weakly.

- ❖ Consider the poor musician who worked all week on an arrangement and then his wife cancelled her weekend trip out of town.

- ❖ Most people don't need to be led into temptation. They can find their own way.

- ❖ Only an Eskimo can keep his wife in the dark for any length of time.

- ❖ Temptation does not create wayward men—it just develops them.

- ❖ Opportunity only knocks, while temptation kicks the door in.

- ❖ Temptation may be strong, but it has never been known to overtake a man running from it.

Love

❖ Some husbands are wonderful. A neighbor, for instance, has been married for ten years and has never stopped being romantic. Of course, if his wife ever finds out about it, she'll probably break his neck.

❖ If your wife no longer gets suspicious when you come home late, it's later than you think. – *Harold Coffin*

❖ My wife just ran off with my best friend and I'm beginning to miss him.

Man vs. Woman

❖ This may be a man's world, but women are partly to blame for the shape it's in.

❖ The man who says he understands women probably doesn't speak the truth about other things, either.

❖ For every woman who makes a fool of a man, there's another who makes a man out of a fool.

❖ An optimist is almost any woman who is on her way to the beauty parlor.

❖ The weaker sex is the stronger sex because of the weakness of the stronger sex for the weaker sex.

❖ When a date's car stalls, a girl should be ready to do likewise. – *Luke Neeley*

❖ If equality of the sexes is ever achieved, it will take men some time to become accustomed to their new rights.

❖ A hen-pecked husband is one who has to fry the bacon after he brings it home.

❖ When a man declares, "I am sure of my wife," it means he is sure of his wife. But when a woman declares, "I am sure of my husband," it means she is sure of herself. – *Francis de Croisset*

❖ The most disillusioned girls are those who married because they were tired of working.

❖ Men don't marry women on $25 a week anymore—a girl must be making at least twice that. – *The Wooden Barrel*

❖ It may be true that wild animals in captivity don't live long, but we know of some married men who have attained a ripe old age.

❖ Equal opportunity is an equal opportunity to prove unequal talents. – *Viscount Samuel*

❖ Men call taking a 50-mile hike training for physical fitness. Women call it shopping.

❖ No man has ever been able to convince his wife that a pretty stenographer is as efficient as an ugly one.

❖ Woman was a side issue at Creation, but the whole works now.

❖ When a man places his wife on a pedestal nowadays, it's probably so she can reach the ceiling with her paint roller.
– *Glenn R. Bernhardt*

❖ Women rule the world by remote control. – *K-Lens-M Komments* (October, 1963)

❖ The blonde down the hall says men may be considered more intelligent than women, but you never see a woman marrying a dumb man because of his shape.

❖ The only female who can tell you everything she's carrying in her bag is a lady kangaroo.

❖ Einstein once said that the instinct governs man's actions. A new substitute for the word wife.

❖ Men would be a lot better off if they stopped trying to understand women and just enjoy them.

❖ Sign in a local paint store: "Husbands selecting colored paints must present notes from their wives."

❖ There are more men in mental hospitals than women. Who's driving whom crazy?

❖ Nowadays a gentleman is one who gives a lady a head start before racing her to a bus seat.

❖ Women and facts are stubborn things. – *K-Lens-M Komments* (April, 1964)

❖ What's wrong with the world is that most born leaders of men are women.

❖ A pessimist is a female who's afraid she won't be able to squeeze her car into a very small parking space. An optimist is a male who thinks she won't try.

❖ Many so-called self-made men just married the right woman and she did the rest.

❖ They tell us there's a new gadget coming out that keeps the inside of a car quiet. It fits tightly over her mouth.

❖ When a woman makes a fool of a man, sometimes it is an improvement.

❖ There's a reason why husbands know all the answers. They have been listening for years.

❖ Anyone who thinks this is a man's world isn't paying attention.

❖ Most husbands have a voice in all domestic affairs. It comes under the heading of a minority report.

❖ Wives of great men remind us of it. – *K-Lens-M Komments* (May, 1965)

❖ The most difficult secret for a man to keep is the opinion he has of himself. – *Marcel Pagnol*

❖ A woman can make a fool of a man in fifteen minutes; but, oh, those fifteen minutes.

❖ All women are mothers of great men—it isn't their fault if life disappoints them later. – *Boris Pasternak*

❖ The biggest problem facing most wives is the one sitting across the table at every meal.

❖ This masculine conclusion is nearly universal: if strength won't budge a sticking drawer, then possibly a curse'll. – *Ruth Chadwick*

❖ The only thing sadder than a "might-have-been" is a "go-getter" who is sorry he gotter.

❖ It's hard to figure out why a girl thinks a man is vulgar and rude because he stares at what she is trying to display.

❖ A wise man is he who has sense enough to cast his lot with a woman who has enough money to build a house on it.

❖ A local girl says life is very confusing. She has to play smart to get a job, but dumb to get a husband.

❖ I told you she was born with a silver foot in her mouth. – *Charles H. Thompson, Jr.*

❖ Boys will be boys, but girls are running them a close race.

❖ About those chicks with bust padding—would you say their statistics have been falsified? – *Earl Wilson*

❖ Women will never be men's equal until they can sport a bald spot on top of their heads and still think they are beautiful.

❖ At long last, thanks to the drip-dry suit, men have equal rights on the shower-curtain rod. – *Bill Vaughan*

❖ When some women claim they've just turned 30, it must be a U-turn. – *Guy Lombardo*

❖ Four out of five woman-haters are women.

❖ If you think your wife respects your judgment, go alone to the department store and buy a new hat for her.

❖ Girls who wear zippers shouldn't live alone. – *John Van Druten*

❖ A fellow told us the other day that his girl was so dumb that she thinks bacteria is the rear entrance to a cafeteria.

❖ A clerk in an office supply store tried to sell a man a letter opener. He said he didn't need one because he married one.

❖ Women can never be as successful as men. They have no wives to advise them.

❖ Men's troubles are usually due to three things: women, money and both.

❖ Definition of a husband: a man who pats his pockets each time he passes a mailbox.

❖ The only way women could have equal rights now would be to surrender some.

❖ Women should make good umpires; a woman never thinks a man's safe when he's out. – *Fred Allen*

❖ The only reason some men make their mark in the world is because their wives made them toe it.

❖ Many a husband has a plunging waistline to match his wife's plunging neckline. – *K-Lens-M Komments* (May, 1964)

❖ A girl can have both a career and a home, if she knows how to put both of them first. – *Grace Downs, Head of a school for models*

❖ Since time began there has never been a conscientious objector in the war between the sexes. – *Dorothy Shay*

❖ A local woman, arguing with her husband, said, "Please shut up! When I want your opinion, I'll give it to you."

❖ It's the weaker sex that puts the caps on jars so tight that the stronger sex can't get them off. — *Earl Wilson*

❖ Many a woman short-changes herself when she marries and expects to improve on the work of nature.

❖ A career woman is one who goes out and earns a man's salary instead of staying at home and taking it away from him.

❖ In some towns the pedestrian legally has the right-of-way. And legally, a husband is the head of the house. Both are safe as long as they don't try to exercise their rights.

❖ If civilization begins over again, will the males regain the upper hand? – *K-Lens-M Komments*

❖ Romance has not changed much through the ages. The ancient Greek gals used to sit in the moonlight and listen to a lyre, too.

❖ Women are now at a disadvantage. Man has finally learned how to travel faster than sound.

❖ On an elevator: "I hate him. He brings out the freckles in me." *– Cedric Adams*

❖ Any wife with an inferiority complex can cure it by being sick in bed for a day while her husband manages the household and the children. *– Eleanor Field*

❖ Girls who try to be walking encyclopedias should remember that reference books are never taken out. *– The Wall Street Journal*

❖ Woman Driver: a person who, when obeying every rule, is blamed for slowing down some man who isn't. *– Marcelene Cox*

❖ When men and women get together at a party, it's usually time to go home. *– Charles Ruffing in Look*

❖ In arguing with a woman a man may have the facts and logic on his side, but the woman has the words.

❖ It's getting so women can do anything men can do—except listen. *– K-Lens-M Komments* (May, 1964)

❖ Anyone can reconcile himself to a woman's having the last word, but some of them never get to it. *– Paul Carruth*

❖ The woman's work that is never done is most likely what she asked her husband to do. *– Franklin P. Jones*

❖ Give a man enough rope and he skips; give a woman enough rope and she makes a marriage knot. *– Louis Ginsberg*

❖ Marriage entitles women to the protection of strong men who steady the ladder while they paint the kitchen.

❖ Women: a delusion men like to hug. – *K-Lens-M Komments*

❖ Men have more problems than women. In the first place, they have to put up with women. – *Francoise Sagan*

❖ Time was when a woman had to carry the wash water from the well, but she didn't sit up half the night trying to figure out how to pay for the bucket.

❖ If your wife wants to learn how to drive, don't stand in her way.

❖ Subordinate: a yard man with bedroom privileges. – *Typo Graphic*

❖ A lot of girls who dish it out can't cook it. – *Vincent Price*

❖ Home cooking is something that most modern women are not. – *Cork, Ireland, Evening Echo*

❖ A woman's head on a man's shoulder often accomplishes more than his does. – *K-Lens-M Komments* (September, 1963)

❖ I asked a Burmese why women, after centuries of following their men, now walk ahead. He said there were many unexploded land mines since the war. – *Robert Mueller*

❖ A husband shouldn't consider himself hen-pecked until he has to wash and iron his own aprons.

❖ Woman, pointing out her home, "That's where we live, the ego and I."

❖ A neighbor was trying to sew on a button. His wife reminded him that the thimble was on the wrong finger. "Yes, I know," he replied, "it should be on yours."

❖ Even if a man could understand women, he still wouldn't believe it. – *Harold Coffin*

❖ Don't do it yourself unless your wife knows how. – *K-Lens-M Komments* (May, 1963)

❖ The easiest way to support a wife in the manner to which she's accustomed is to let her keep her job. – *Franklin P. Jones*

❖ Wives, like children, need to be loved most when they least deserve it. – *Dr. Paul Popenoe*

❖ If equality of the sexes is ever achieved, it will take men quite some time to become used to their new rights.

❖ Most men would do less lying if their wives refrained from asking questions.

❖ Although man has learned through evolution to walk in an upright position, his eyes still swing from limb to limb. – *Margaret Schooley*

❖ A statistician tells us that millions of women are getting men's wages nowadays. Was there ever a time when they didn't?

❖ When you see a man opening the door of an automobile for his wife, you can be sure that either the automobile or the wife is new. – *Paul Gibson*

❖ Behind every successful man is a woman who certainly surprised his mother. – *Dan Bennett*

❖ To those fellows who are constantly bragging that they wear the pants in their families, we would suggest that they protect them by wearing aprons while doing the dishes.

❖ For one who never knows what she wants, my wife's surprisingly adept at getting it. – *Charles Chan*

❖ One thing men can't understand about women is how women understand so much about men. – *Walt Streightiff*

❖ The battle of the sexes will never be won by either side; there is too much fraternizing with the enemy. – *Anonymous*

❖ A woman has two chances to a man's one of becoming a success. If she can't get what she wants by being smart, she can usually get it by being dumb. – *Mildred Miller*

❖ Matrimony: only state allowing women to work 18 hours a day. – *K-Lens-M Komments*

Surprising Facts by K-Lens-M Komments

✓ The U.S. has 4,000,000 more women than men. (March, 1964)
✓ Women read more than men. (May, 1964)
✓ The average woman knows and uses more words than the average man. (October, 1965)

Men

- A sweet young thing recently told us that wolves are like railroad trains; you like to hear the whistle even if you don't want to go any place.

- A man is as young as he feels after trying to prove it.

- Sooner or later every husband catches the common scold.

- Whenever a man gets too set in his ways, he stumbles over himself to get anywhere.

- Experience proves that the easier it is to reform a man the oftener the job has to be done.

- The world gives a man an alternative. He can either stand up and be counted or lie down and be counted out.

- Example of poor distribution: bald-headed man with a mustache.

- For fixing things around the house, nothing beats a man who is handy with a checkbook.

- As long as there are bald-headed men, there'll always be a market for hats.

- Looking at it from a practical point of view, it is the average man who occupies the most useful places in life.

- Praise is better than wheat germ for even the least vain of men, and every wife ought to keep a supply in her pocket ready to scatter like manna. – *Phyllis McGinley*

❖ We have heard it said that every man is a fool for at least five minutes each day. The real danger is in exceeding the time limit.

❖ Jonah's experience with the whale proves that you can't keep a good man down.

❖ Find a man who is satisfied with things as they come, and you can be sure he doesn't expect much.

❖ Man is but a worm. He comes along, wiggles a bit, and then some chicken gets him. – *Grit*

❖ Barbershop Quartet: vocalamity. – *K-Lens-M Komments* (March, 1964)

❖ Even though a man does change his mind, he has never been known to get a better one.

❖ Bachelor: a man who thinks a weekend is something you rest up in. – *Ken Kraft*

❖ A man who trims himself to suit everybody will soon whittle himself away. –*Charles Schwab*

❖ A wise girl will hitch her wagon to a man who works like a horse.

❖ Has anyone ever seen a man get on a bus ahead of a short skirt?

❖ No man is indispensible—the world was here first. – *K-Lens-M Komments*

❖ It is estimated that the average man has twelve million brain cells—most of them unemployed.

❖ A man is like an egg. If kept continually in hot water, he will get hard boiled.

❖ Man is nothing but dust, and a woman sure can handle him.

❖ Men are like the steel girders of a skyscraper. The ones you don't see do most of the supporting.

❖ A man will always pay a fancy figure for checking his hat.
– *Usher F. Newlin*

❖ A man will never amount to much if he is known only by the deeds of his ancestors.

❖ The self-made man has one fault: he is not self-contained.

❖ I always like to hear a man talk about himself, because then I never hear anything but good. – *Will Rogers*

❖ Man's worst ill is his stubbornness of heart.

❖ Imagination was given to a man to compensate him for what he is not, and a sense of humor was provided to console him for what he is.

❖ The man who lets go of himself has one way to go—down.

❖ One thing most men can do better than anybody else is to read their own handwriting.

❖ Men are like wines; age souring the bad and bettering the good.
– *Cicero.*

❖ I don't mind living in a man's world as long as I can be a woman in it. – *Marilyn Monroe*

❖ Men know how to make it rain, but there are still some who don't know enough to come in out of it.

❖ One nice thing about being a man is that you don't have to kiss someone who hasn't shaved for two or three days.

❖ He has a one-track mind—and a dirt track, at that.
– *George Baker*

❖ Nothing is enough for the man to whom enough is too little.
– *Epicurus*

❖ We suppose there is hardly a man who has not an apple orchard tucked away in his heart somewhere. – *Christopher Morley*

❖ Guess it is just human nature that most men are more interested in getting their bite than in giving their bit.

❖ One of the marks of a gentleman is never to show that he's tired.
– *E. V. Lucas*

❖ Bachelor: a man who has faults he doesn't know about.
– *Franklin P. Jones*

❖ There are so many ways of being a fool that no man can dodge them all.

❖ When a man is resigned to his fate, his resignation is usually accepted.

❖ Bald-headed men usually have serene dispositions—nothing ever gets in their hair.

❖ A real man is he whose goodness is a part of himself.

❖ The ideal man bears the accidents of life with dignity and grace, making the best of the circumstances. – *Aristotle*

❖ If the self-satisfied man could only see himself as others do.

❖ There are only three kinds of men: underage, overage and average.

❖ If we didn't have the little men in the world, the great men would never be noticed.

❖ To be opposed by certain types of men is the best evidence that you really amount to something.

❖ Wolf: a man of single purpose and double talk. – *Dan Bennett*

Mistakes & Experience

❖ Never make the same mistake twice. Vary it a little—you'll feel better.

❖ He who takes time to explain his mistakes has little time left for anything else.

❖ One reason why we miss so many opportunities is that they look so much bigger going than they did coming.

❖ Experience may be the best teacher, but she never finds an apple on her desk.

❖ The only person who never makes a mistake is one who never does anything.

❖ Architects cover their mistakes with ivy, doctors with sod, and wives with mayonnaise.

❖ You don't profit from the mistakes you make in the stock market. – *K-Lens-M Komments* (August, 1963)

❖ Lucky guesses may pass for good judgment, but don't bank on them.

❖ Pay for your experiences, but always carry the receipt with you.

❖ Don't judge a man's future by his past. Experience may have taught him a lesson.

❖ Experience is what makes you wonder how it got a reputation for being the best teacher. – *Franklin P. Jones*

❖ Nonchalance: the ability to look like an owl when you have acted like a jackass. – *Santa Fe Magazine*

❖ The fellow who lives to learn will soon learn to live.

❖ Experience may be a good teacher, but every time a man stoops to pick up a few cents' worth, he drops a dollar.

❖ Profit from your past mistakes is non-taxable. – *K-Lens-M Komments* (October, 1965)

❖ Accomplishments are the results of mistakes that you have corrected over and over again.

❖ It seldom happens that man errs through an excess of moderation.

❖ If you live it up, chances are you will have to live it down.

❖ Experience is that which recognizes a mistake the second time you make it.

❖ To err is human—but generally a much better excuse is demanded.

❖ How nice it would be to retire in old age if a man could sell his experience for what it cost him.

❖ Smart people speak from experience—but smarter people, from experience, don't speak.

❖ The worth of experience depends entirely upon the after effects.

❖ Experience is still the best teacher. An added advantage is that you get individual instruction. – *Lloyd Burns*

❖ Good judgment comes from experience and experience comes from bad judgment.

❖ Inexperience is the best teacher. – *K-Lens-M Komments* (October, 1963)

❖ Experience teaches a lot of people a lot of things they didn't want to learn.

❖ A mistake at least proves somebody stopped talking long enough to do something. – *Phoenix Flame*

❖ The only thing some people learn from experience is that they made another mistake.

❖ We frequently use the term *tough luck* to cover up poor judgment.

❖ Experience is one thing that is never a good secondhand buy.

❖ There are no erasers for mistakes in judgment.

❖ Making a mistake is only half as bad as making an excuse for it. – *Ron Butler*

❖ The man who is afraid to admit his mistakes is making another.

❖ We learn from experience not to make the same mistake again. Then we try a new way of getting into trouble.

❖ Experience is a fancy name we use when speaking of past blunders.

❖ Snub: slight mistake. – *K-Lens-M Komments* (October, 1963)

❖ Don't laugh at others' mistakes; it may be your turn next.

❖ Experience is what keeps a man who makes the same mistake twice from admitting it a third time around. – *Terry McCormick*

❖ If you're smart, you'll learn from the mistakes of others. You can't possibly live long enough to make them all yourself.

❖ Experience may be a thorough teacher, but no man lives long enough to graduate.

❖ Take time to look back occasionally; some useful lessons may be learned from past errors.

❖ A man must have experience before he can be a shoemaker, but it seems that he needs no judicial experience to become a judge of a high court.

❖ Experience comes fast to the fellow who tries to have a big time on very little money.

❖ The height of unimportance is that sensation you have when you make a mistake and nobody notices it.

❖ The best substitute for experience is being about sixteen. – *K-Lens-M Komments* (August, 1963)

❖ To cover up a mistake doesn't mean that you have accomplished something.

❖ If experience is a good teacher, many people have a liberal education.

❖ Experience is a poor guide to man, and is seldom followed. What really teaches a man is not experience, but observation. – *H. L. Mencken*

❖ Those who make the most mistakes find it easy to make excuses.

❖ In the school of experience the faculty changes, but the lessons stay the same.

❖ Experience: a school where a man learns what a big fool he has been. – *Josh Billings*

❖ Proverbs are the daughters of daily experience.

❖ Experience is the sum total of a man's blunders.

❖ You feel more pain in the dark—especially when you stub your toe. – *K-Lens-M Komments*

❖ The best inventors are those who invent excuses for their own failures.

❖ Broadmindedness is highmindedness flattened out by experience. – *Clipper*

❖ Experience may be the best teacher, but she is often late for school.

❖ The school of experience charges most for its night courses. – *K-Lens-M Komments* (August, 1965)

Money

❖ The only attachment that fits all cars is the finance company.

❖ Modern man is one who drives a mortgaged car over a bond-financed highway on credit card gas.

❖ 'Tis much better to tighten your belt in a recession than to lose your pants in a panic.

❖ It is better to live in extreme poverty than to be able to buy every luxury except a clear conscience.

❖ All some save of their salary is the envelope. – *K-Lens-M Komments* (October, 1965)

❖ The world accepts the rule of gold rather than the golden rule.

❖ Most people imagine their troubles would end if they were paid all the money they are worth.

❖ Love of money keeps many people out of trouble by keeping them busy earning it.

❖ People who contribute large sums of money to charity usually manage to get caught in the act.

❖ Most people don't care how much they pay for something, as long as it's not all at once. – *Terry Zerbe*

❖ The world is so full of a number of things that it's hard to keep up payments on them. – *McLeansboro, Illinois, Time-Leader*

❖ Jack Benny to Jayne Mansfield: "You look like a million bucks, and that's quite a lot—about $116,000 after taxes.
– *Erskine Johnson*

❖ People who have had occasion to hire a lawyer are very hard to convince that talk is cheap.

❖ Put your property in your wife's name before starting out to beat the other fellow at his own game.

❖ Nothing seems to need more fixing than a fixed income.

❖ If you want to see a short summer, borrow some money due in the fall.

❖ The eagle on the American dollar should be replaced with a homing pigeon. – *K-Lens-M Komments*

❖ The definition of inflation: something that cost $10.00 a few years ago and now costs $15.00 to fix.

❖ The money the other fellow has is capital; getting it away from him is labor.

❖ Even if money could buy happiness, think what a luxury tax there would be on it.

❖ The most expensive part of poverty comes from trying to hide it.

❖ Great wealth doesn't buy happiness. It only helps you look for it in interesting places.

❖ Nothing makes your old homes look attractive as pricing the new ones.

❖ Some people might reduce by living within their incomes.

❖ Even if you have money to burn, you can't take it with you.

❖ The best way to save money is to spend it well.

❖ When it comes to picking up the check, he has an impediment in his reach. – *E. Simms Campbell*

❖ Money blown in on a wet night might better have been saved for a rainy day.

❖ About the only thing that will keep bills down these days is a paperweight.

❖ The cleanest thing in the world is a dollar bill. Not even a germ can live on a dollar these days.

❖ Twenty years ago, lots of folks dreamed about earning the salary they can't get along on today.

❖ People are paid wages for doing things they are told to do, and salaries for doing the same things without being told.

❖ Income tax is the fine you pay for reckless thriving.

❖ A tightrope walker lost his life recently. He was tight, but the rope wasn't.

❖ If you want to make money fast, glue it to the floor.

❖ If you make out your income tax report correctly, you go to the poorhouse; if not you go to jail.

Money

❖ Lack of cash in his pocket controls a man more firmly than his principles.

❖ The best things in life may be free, but it takes a little hard cash to point them in your direction.

❖ The more wealth some people accumulate, the less they think others are entitled to.

❖ Money isn't everything, but it's way ahead of whatever is in second place. – *Gordon Gammack*

❖ Rags make paper; paper makes money; money makes banks; banks make loans; loans make poverty; poverty makes rags. 'Round and 'round she goes, and we're right back where we started.

❖ An estimate is a rough idea of how rough the cost will be.

❖ For every man who gets rich quick, there are dozens of others who get poor even quicker.

❖ People who complain about paying income taxes may be divided into two classes—men and women.

❖ One thing inflation has done is that it enables a person to brag about having paid an enormous price for something without lying about it.

❖ A banker offers his analysis of time: yesterday is a canceled check, tomorrow is a promissory note, today is ready cash; spend it wisely.

❖ The reward for saving your money is being able to pay your taxes without borrowing.

❖ Living on a budget is the same as living beyond your means except that you have a record of it. – *Carl Ellstam*

❖ About the only thing that money cannot buy is poverty.

❖ Today's big problem: how to lift a mortgage while riding in it.

❖ Inflation is being broke with a lot of money in your pocket. – *Industrial Press Service*

❖ In the good old days, the man who saved money was a miser; now he's a genius.

❖ Income tax expert: someone whose fee is the amount he saves you in making out your taxes. – *Contributed by Dan Bennett*

❖ There's something even handier than a credit card. It eliminates waiting, ends billing, is honored everywhere. It is called money. – *Changing Times, The Kiplinger Magazine*

❖ Hard cash – the softest thing to fall back on.

❖ The principle export of the United States is money.

❖ Inflation means that by the time the boss gets around to giving that promised raise, it won't be enough.

❖ It is quite possible to cash in on good resolutions—if you keep them long enough to earn dividends.

❖ There is a difference between a sound investment and one that sounds good.

❖ Poverty may be a virtue, but it has never furnished a home.

❖ We should be thankful that we don't go broke as easily as our good intentions.

❖ There's only one thing you can get for a nickel nowadays—five pennies. – *Ralph Hawkins*

❖ Old bankers never die—they just lose interest.

❖ All you can do on a shoestring is trip. – *K-Lens-M Komments* (August, 1963)

❖ Economy is a very much neglected source of revenue.

❖ A man pays a luxury tax on his billfold, an income tax on the stuff he puts into it, and a sales tax whenever he takes anything out.

❖ In the frantic search for riches, many lose sight of the things that money will never buy.

❖ We are now living in the electrical age—just about everything is charged.

❖ A necessity is a luxury you can buy on the installment plan.

❖ A man may have more money than brains—but not for long.

❖ Inflation: tipping more than you once paid for a meal. – *K-Lens-M Komments* (August, 1964)

❖ A fool and his money are soon parted. Nowadays you don't even have to be a fool.

❖ Money saved for a rainy day buys a much smaller umbrella than it used to.

❖ A dollar in the hand is worth more than the hundred you expect to borrow.

❖ The trouble with the installment plan is that, by the time you get something paid for, it is obsolete.

❖ The advantage of being broke is that it doesn't take much to improve the situation.

❖ Ours is the only country in the world where a man can fill a three-car garage with automobiles he doesn't own.

❖ One thing about the color of money is it never clashes with any outfit a person is wearing.

❖ The whole question of economics can be boiled down to a single sentence, "There is no free lunch."

❖ Even the man who feels he has nothing to live for finds that he can't live for nothing today.

❖ Money will buy a dog, but only love will make him wag his tail.

❖ This country doesn't need new money, just more power to the old.

❖ When bills are too numerous, it's hard to find life humorous. – *K-Lens-M Komments* (August, 1964)

❖ They say some people can't stand prosperity, however, the rest of us would like a try at it.

❖ There was a time when a fool and his money were soon parted. Now it happens to everybody. – *Arejas Vitkauskas*

❖ The man who has more money than brains, usually needs it.

❖ Collateral is something you have to show at the bank to prove you don't need the money you want to borrow.

❖ At 20, I wanted to save the world. Now I'd be satisfied just to save part of my salary. – *Earl Wilson*

❖ Trying to keep up with the Joneses has drowned many a man in red ink.

❖ It may be true that nowadays money goes a little further on some items, but it still won't stretch from payday to payday.

❖ When quality is sacrificed to economy, there is no economy.

❖ What the man who has everything needs is help with the payments. – *Maurice Seitter*

❖ Money is something you should make first and then make last.

❖ A fool and his money are soon investigated. – *K-Lens-M Komments* (April, 1964)

❖ A dollar won't do nearly so much as it used to, but remember that hardly anything else does, either.

❖ Some housewives go over their budgets carefully; others just go over them.

❖ Time is money, but not to the man who spends a dollar's worth of time trying to save a penny.

❖ One good thing about inflation is that nowadays it is impossible for a kid to get sick on a five-cent candy bar.

❖ Nothing makes people go into debt like trying to keep up with those who are already in up to their necks.

- ❖ He who hesitates may be spending his own money.
  – K-Lens-M Komments (August, 1963)

- ❖ To be sound as a dollar these days means you are half dead.

- ❖ The problems of life consist mostly of subtracting what a man owns from what he owes.

- ❖ We are better off financially if we act our wage.

- ❖ Save your money if you can. It may be worth something again some day.

- ❖ Two can live as cheaply as one, but they both show it.

- ❖ Money may not buy happiness, but it certainly lets you look for it in a lot more places.

- ❖ Here's a verse that ain't too funny: Too much month at the end of the money.

- ❖ If you can expect a rebate from the high cost of living, brother, you are an optimist.

- ❖ A fine is a tax you have to pay for doing wrong. A tax is a fine you have to pay for doing okay.

- ❖ A budget's like a one-way street—both ends never seem to meet.
  – K-Lens-M Komments (July, 1964)

- ❖ A forger is a guy who gives a check a bad name.

- ❖ Sometimes it seems that charity has been commercialized until all the sweetness has been squeezed out of it.

- ❖ The fellow with money to burn seldom has to beg for a match.

❖ The toughest assignment in the world is to try to convince a self-made man that he cheated himself.

❖ People have stopped worrying about taking their money with them. The problem is making it stretch while they are here.

❖ The wages of sin is debt. – *K-Lens-M Komments* (May, 1965)

❖ Being able to hold on to money doesn't always mean a man is stronger. It may mean that he is single.

❖ You can't tell how happy a man is by the amount of money he has. A man with two million dollars may be just as happy as one with eleven million.

❖ Usually the fellow with money to burn lives to rake the ashes.

❖ Many people who have more money than they know what to do with are mighty short in some other departments.

❖ Money's not everything, but it takes the fright out of reading menus from left to right. – *K-Lens-M Komments* (September, 1963)

❖ Money talks, but seldom gets chummy with the average man.

❖ A budget is a bunch of figures that prove you shouldn't have gotten married in the first place.

❖ One of life's biggest problems seems to be how to make money and friends at the same time.

❖ Today's dime is really a dollar with the taxes taken out.

❖ Money sure comes in handy when you've misplaced your credit cards.

❖ Money is a mask—it makes some vices look like virtues.

❖ There was a time when ten cents would buy much more, but dimes have changed.

❖ Money isn't a problem—it's the answer. – *K-Lens-M Komments* (May, 1965)

❖ A child who knows the value of a dollar these days must be mighty discouraged. – *Earl Wilson*

❖ Money talks—and when it does few people need hearing aids.

❖ That he deserves all he gets is seldom said of a man who is making a million dollars.

❖ Money cannot buy friends, but it can give you a better class of enemies.

❖ No man is a hero to his wallet. – *K-Lens-M Komments* (May, 1965)

❖ It's a funny thing about money. Men get their faces on it but women get their hands on it.

❖ Money talks, but these days the dollar doesn't have enough cents to say anything.

❖ Inflation: a fate worse than debt. – *K-Lens-M Komments* (May, 1964)

❖ Mixed greens are good for you — especially those fives, tens, and twenties.

❖ Some people have made an art of being slow to pick up the check. You've really got to hand it to them.

❖ Put too many dollars in the wrong man's hands and it crowds out the sense in his head.

❖ Meeting your bills is no problem—they're eager to meet you.
  – *K-Lens-M Komments* (August, 1965)

❖ In a loan company office: "Ask us about our plans for owning
  your home." – *Art Ryon*

❖ Money still talks, but who wants to listen to a one-sided
  conversation?

❖ A fool and his money get along as well as anybody these days.

❖ Many a wallet would be flatter if you removed the credit cards.
  – *K-Lens-M Komments* (August, 1963)

❖ Running into debt isn't so bad; it's running into your creditors
  that's so very embarrassing.

❖ It's the cost of high living that lays many a family low.

❖ Capital is only the fruit of labor and could never have existed if
  labor had not first existed. – *Abraham Lincoln*

❖ Nothing makes people go into debt like trying to keep up with
  people who already are.

❖ It's tough to pay as you go and still not go anywhere. – *K-Lens-M
  Komments*

❖ The old woman who lived in a shoe now has a lot of descendants
  who are living on a shoestring. – *Mont Hurst*

❖ It's hard to get rich in a small town—everybody's watching.
  – *K-Lens-M Komments* (July, 1964)

❖ Most of us have our ups and downs and some never pay up until
  they are run down.

❖ Inflation: when what goes up must go up. – *K–Lens–M Komments*

❖ It's a depression when even people who don't intend to pay quit buying.

❖ A joint checking account is never overdrawn by the wife. It is just under deposited by the husband.

❖ Money isn't anything, but it's the best substitute there is for credit.

❖ Poise is the ability to talk fluently while the other fellow is paying the check.

❖ Gentleman farmer: a man with more hay in the bank than in the bar. – *Earl Wilson*

❖ The way food prices are going up, it will soon be cheaper to eat the money.

❖ At a service station on road leaving Las Vegas: "Free aspirin and tender sympathy." – *Mrs. R. V. Smiley*

❖ No matter what the economists say, we all know what causes inflation: too much money going to somebody else. – *Bill Vaughan*

❖ Here's a sure cure for money ills: the new mailbox that rejects bills. – *K–Lens–M Komments* (July, 1964)

❖ Money may not grow on trees, but the man who buys lumber today could easily believe in the myth.

❖ Money may not bring real happiness, but many will say the imitation is almost perfect.

❖ Bank account: here today and drawn tomorrow. – *Hal Raymond*

❖ By the time a family acquires a nest egg these days, inflation has turned it into chicken feed. – *Business Briefs*

❖ While money isn't everything, it does keep you in touch with your children. –*Changing Times, The Kiplinger Magazine*

❖ Back in the days when a dollar would buy twice as much as it does now, you probably didn't have one.

❖ If the family budget looks sick at the end of the month, it may be something you ate.

❖ If money talks, it speaks the mother tongue. – *K-Lens-M Komments* (August, 1965)

❖ Early to bed and early to rise, until you make enough money to do otherwise.

❖ Money doesn't go far, but what it lacks in distance is made up in space.

❖ Taxpayer: a person who has the government on his payroll. – *O. A. Battista*

❖ Budget: a system of reminding yourself that you can't afford the kind of living you've grown accustomed to. – *Changing Times, The Kiplinger Magazine*

❖ Several companies sell fine adding machines, but in the field of subtraction the slot machine is tops.

❖ Costrophobia: fear of high prices. – *K-Lens-M Komments* (July, 1964)

❖ The trouble with today's dollar is that it seems to have been built more for speed than for endurance.

❖ Statistics indicate that the average family could use more money than it is getting—and usually does. – *Vesta M. Kelly*

❖ Money in need is a friend indeed. – *K-Lens-M Komments* (April, 1964)

❖ America is the country where it takes more brains to make out the income-tax return than it does to make the income. – *Evan Eser*

❖ Money may not be everything, but there are times when only cost can pull us out of a hole.

❖ Trying for a killing may not leave enough time to make a living.

❖ It's becoming the I.O.U.S.A. – *K-Lens-M Komments* (May, 1965)

❖ The greatest drawback to economy is that very few people ever save money by practicing it.

❖ Many folks have quit worrying about how to spend the money they earn and now worry about earning the money they spend.

❖ It's darkest before you've overdrawn. – *K-Lens-M Komments* (May, 1965)

❖ Sometimes labor is on top and sometimes capital is, but there is never any doubt as to who is in the middle. – *Dan Bennett*

❖ Money causes a lot of trouble, but many people are looking for trouble anyway.

❖ Don't make it the purse-suit of happiness. – *K-Lens-M Komments*

❖ Inflation: when people who used to say money isn't everything say it's hardly anything. – *Fletcher Knebel*

❖ Poverty may be no crime, but it has a penalty just the same.

Surprising Facts by K-Lens-M Komments

- ✓ Men tip twice as much as women. (April, 1964)
- ✓ A worn dollar will make a good (lintless) eyeglass cleaner. (July, 1964)
- ✓ Over 300,000 U.S. insurance policies are lost, mutilated or stolen each year. (August, 1965)

People

❖ There's so much good in the worst of us and so much bad in the best of us, that it's hard to tell which one of us should be the one to reform the rest of us.

❖ Many folks can best make their presence felt by their absence.

❖ The loudest barkers are always with the sideshow—never with the main attraction.

❖ Critics burn the candor at both ends. – *K-Lens-M Komments* (October, 1965)

❖ People who sympathize with themselves have outlived their usefulness.

❖ Egotism is the art of seeing in yourself the qualities that no one else can see.

❖ Two half-wits do not make a wit.

❖ Well-balanced people are those who are not easily upset.

❖ Lots of people get credit for having personality when actually they're just proud of their teeth.

❖ Idle gossip never is. – *K-Lens-M Komments* (October, 1965)

❖ Most people can keep a secret. It's the folks they tell it to who can't.

People

❖ People who live in glass houses are interesting neighbors.

❖ Some people are born with black eyes; others have to fight for them.

❖ The average man is one who thinks he isn't.

❖ Pickpocket: quick change artist. – *K-Lens-M Komments* (October, 1965)

❖ People who talk to themselves hear a lot of compliments.

❖ Loose conduct gets many people in a tight spot.

❖ A lot of people can rise to the occasion, but few know when to sit down.

❖ A fountain is water getting up in the air and making a prettier spectacle of itself than people who do likewise.

❖ Unless you feed their ego, some folks won't stay. – *K-Lens-M Komments* (August, 1964)

❖ The world is full of seekers—some looking for trouble and others finding fault.

❖ Some people preach charity and wait for others to practice it.

❖ People who expect to have their own way must resent it if it is unfavorable.

❖ A sympathizer is a fellow who's for you as long as it doesn't cost him anything.

❖ Folks who like to be waited on are the hardest ones to be cured of their ailments.

❖ Good neighbor: one talking to you, not about you. – *K-Lens-M Komments* (March, 1964)

❖ Superior people talk about ideas; average people talk about things; and little people talk about other people.

❖ Some people go through a stage that lasts their entire life. – *K-Lens-M Komments* (October, 1963)

❖ A stuffed shirt is usually all front.

❖ A good sport will always let you have your own way.

❖ Pacifists are people who permit others to fight their battles.

❖ Men are judged by their actions, women by their looks, and mules and onions by their strength.

❖ Toupees are made for men who have nothing to hide.

❖ Some people can't unbend and be human until misfortune comes and takes the starch out of them.

❖ If thoughts could be read, faces might be redder. – *K-Lens-M Komments* (August, 1964)

❖ Neurotic: sweetheart of Sigmund Freud. – *Paul H. Gilbert*

❖ A gentleman is one who holds the door while his wife carries in the groceries.

❖ In certain circles, many black sheep are whitewashed.

❖ Some people's idea of harmony is to have things their own way.

❖ It costs more to feed most people's pride than their faces.

❖ Peace will never come to the peacemaker who butts in.

❖ Faultfinders are usually familiar with a microscope, but seldom look into a mirror.

❖ Some people are good losers—others can't act. – *K-Lens-M Komments* (June, 1962)

❖ A perfectionist is one who never quite finishes what he starts to do.

❖ After a man starts going bad, he doesn't need to be shown the way.

❖ It's not a cheaper car that people want; it's an expensive car that costs less. – *Changing Times, The Kiplinger Magazine.*

❖ It takes all kinds of people to make a world, but a lot of them don't help much.

❖ A bore is a person who never tries to make a long story short.

❖ The more you think of some people, the less you think of them.

❖ A liar is a verbal cripple. – *K-Lens-M Komments* (May, 1965)

❖ A lot of people get discovered—others just get found out.

❖ There are many people in the world who will keep everything except their promises.

❖ Some of the most disappointed people in the world are the ones who get what's coming to them.

❖ Rumors are nothing more than a breeze made up by a couple of windbags.

❖ Folks would get along better if they could get up steam as easily as they generate hot air.

❖ Bore: a person who arrives dragging his tale behind him.
  – *Edith Ogutsch*

❖ In the business world, an executive knows something about everything, a technician knows everything about something, and the switchboard operator knows everything. – *Harold Coffin*

❖ Gossips have been catalogued in three different types: the vest-button type – always popping off; the vacuum cleaner types – always picking up the dirty; the liniment type – always rubbing it in.

❖ Hitchhiker: digital commuter. – *Mary Markley*

❖ Some are bent from toil; others grow crooked trying to avoid it.

❖ Many people don't like to repeat gossip, but what else can you do with it?

❖ Maybe you can't fool all the people all the time, but leave them alone and a great many will fool themselves.

❖ Most people find it a lot easier to talk than to think.

❖ A good neighbor is one who can watch you take it easy without thinking you are lazy.

❖ Some people do not have to fly very high to live up to their ideals.

❖ A ringleader is the first one in the bathtub.

People

- ❖ Some heads are like doorknobs—anybody can turn them.

- ❖ One thing's certain. We may differ now but when we get to the cemetery, we'll be on the same level.

- ❖ Schizophrenia: a state in which two people can live as cheaply as one. – *Robert Williams*

- ❖ This old world needs fewer busybodies and more bodies busy.

- ❖ This would be a fine world if all men showed as much patience all the time as they do when waiting for a fish to bite.

- ❖ A Bostonian is an American, broadly speaking.

- ❖ A snake, an alligator and a gossip are harmless as long as they keep their mouths closed.

- ❖ Gossip peddlers might appropriately be called misfortune tellers.

- ❖ People seldom forget the names or faces of others whom they think it may pay to know.

- ❖ The quickest way to get people interested in a project is to tell them that it is none of their business.

- ❖ Marilyn Monroe: a girl you look up to, very, very slowly. – *Sammy Kaye*

- ❖ Sometimes the only thing that keeps the human race going seems to be the lack of parking spaces.

- ❖ Some girls who can't be forced into cleaning up the house are great at picking up all the dirt in the neighborhood.

❖ Fortune hunter: "I love the ground she walks on, and the property she owns on the other side of town, too." – *Red Skelton*

❖ Bore: one whose shortcoming is his long-staying.

❖ Some people cast reflections just to show how brilliant they are.

❖ Many folks' worst fault seems to be trying to tell other people of theirs.

❖ People who tell everything they hear often add a little more.

❖ "He's a VIB—a very important bore." – *New York World-Telegram and The Sun*

❖ Some people have as their motto: "If you can't say anything good about a person, let's hear it." – *Maurice Seitter*

❖ Critic: one who finds a little bad in the best of things.
   – *Joseph P. Ritz*

❖ Of every ten persons who speak about you, nine will say something bad, and the tenth will say something good in a bad way.

❖ Many a man is enough of a dope to be easily cleaned by the use of soft soap. – *Hal Chadwick*

❖ Some people don't put their best foot forward until they get the other one in hot water.

❖ Some people can't tell right from wrong until they are found out.

❖ Gossip never has trouble finding its way around, even in a strange neighborhood.

❖ Neurotic: a person who can't leave being well enough alone.
 – *Dan Bennett*

❖ The right man in the right place is sure not to be left.

❖ Isn't it odd how neighbors whom we seldom see all winter
 write to wish we were with them when they get 500 miles away?

❖ He's got a lot of depth on the surface, but deep down he's
 shallow.

❖ Some people have so many irons in the fire and change them so
 often that only the handles get hot.

❖ Diversity helps us endure adversity. – *K-Lens–M Komments*
 (April, 1964)

❖ Beauty parlor: where the talk alone is enough to curl your hair.
 – *Luke Neely*

❖ Accept a favor from some people and you place a mortgage on
 your peace of mind.

❖ Self-made women will never replace self-made men. They
 change their minds too often.

❖ Some people wait until they are out on a limb before they turn
 over a new leaf.

❖ These days, the fellow who keeps saying there's nothing to
 worry about is the one we should worry about.

❖ None are so blind that they cannot see the faults of others.

❖ Most people will buy anything that is marked only one to a
 customer.

❖ Bouncer: a fellow who stands ready to help you out.
 – *K-Lens-M Komments* (August, 1965)

❖ Men tire themselves in pursuit of rest. – *Laurence Stern*

❖ For some people, fun begins where common sense leaves off.

❖ Flappers are like brown sugar. They are sweet but refined.

❖ There seems to be no cure for blindness to our own
 imperfections. – *K-Lens-M Komments* (May, 1964)

❖ A man is far different from a machine in that he is seldom
 quiet when well oiled.

❖ Fear of being found out keeps a lot of people on the straight
 and narrow path.

❖ Gossip: a person who puts two and two together—whether
 they are or not. – *Mary McCoy*

❖ A pessimist is a man so confused he tries to go full speed
 ahead in reverse.

❖ When a person is bad, we are sorry; but there is a way of being
 good that bores us to distraction.

❖ The world is filled with people who are anxious to function
 in an advisory capacity. – *Charles Schulz*

❖ Psychiatrist: a mental Peeping Tom. – *K-Lens-M Komments*

❖ Some people have plenty of push when it comes to shoving
 others in the wrong direction.

❖ The memories that seem to last the longest with some people are the shortcomings of their acquaintances.

❖ Sophisticated people are those who can do naughty things without feeling guilty.

❖ It's easy enough to spot a bore—he talks like a revolving door.
  – *K-Lens-M Komments*

❖ Hypocrisy is the tribute vice pays to virtue.
  – *Kenneth W. Thompson*

❖ Even though they do not have a leg to stand on, rumors have a way of getting around.

❖ Some people find fault as if it were buried somewhere.
  – *Francis O'Walsh*

❖ No man is worth much to his community until he learns to make the most of himself.

❖ History proves that human nature can be improved a little, but has never been radically changed.

❖ Gossip: her say. – *K-Lens-M Komments* (September, 1963)

❖ Why is it that most people want the front of the bus, the back of the church, and the middle of the road? – *Ruby Ingraham*

❖ A cynic is a man who has sized himself up and then got sore about it.

❖ Gossip: one who burns the scandal at both ends.
  – *K-Lens-M Komments* (August, 1963)

❖ When a man puts up a bluff, he's trying to cover up the fact that he can't deliver the goods he promised.

❖ Too many people believe only half they hear—the wrong half.

❖ The only time some folks follow the straight and narrow path is in a supermarket. – *K-Lens-M Komments*

❖ The only exercise some people get is jumping at conclusions, running down their friends, side-stepping responsibility and pushing their luck. – *Arnold H. Glasgow*

❖ The rising generation may be rising, but it's mighty hard to get it out of bed.

❖ Some people keep a secret in loose-lipped form.

❖ Gossip peddlers find that the easiest way to make a mountain out of a molehill is to add a little dirt.

❖ A cocktail party is where you meet friends you never saw before.

❖ Of course silence is golden. The other fellow's, we mean.

❖ Hypocrite: one who claims he isn't. – *K-Lens-M Komments* (May, 1963)

❖ A miracle man is one who can weather an attack of love and wisdom at the same time.

❖ There are people who make things happen, people who watch things happen, and people who don't know anything happened. – *Gordon, Nebraska, Journal*

❖ Some folks are like fences; they run around a lot without getting anywhere.

❖ Some people never get enough. Do them a favor and they expect an encore.

❖ Juries sometimes fail to convict on circumstantial evidence, but the neighbors never do.

❖ People with no business of their own sometimes cause the man who has one to fail.

❖ When it comes to doing for others, some people stop at nothing. – *General Features Corp.*

❖ Chicken and people are alike in that the more you give them the less they scratch for themselves.

❖ Eavesdropper: one who gets in your hear. – *K-Lens-M Komments* (August, 1965)

❖ A gentleman is a man who leaves the lawn mower and garden tools out where his wife can find them.

❖ One of our toughest problems is how to be tolerant with an intolerant person.

❖ Immortality is the genius to move others long after you yourself have stopped moving. – *Frank Rooney*

❖ Critic: a person who tells us what we like. – *K-Lens-M Komments* (May, 1963)

❖ The world would be in much worse shape if some men preached what they practice.

❖ The man whose great-grandfather found his way across the continent traveling over a trackless waste, nowadays gets lost in a supermarket.

❖ A critic is a wet blanket that soaks everything it touches.

❖ Too many people are taking advantage of the fact that it isn't human to be perfect.

❖ We will not be honored for what we receive, but rather for what we give.

❖ Gossip: a person with a sense of rumor.

❖ The people to fear are not those who disagree with you, but those who disagree with you and are too cowardly to let you know. — *Napoleon*

❖ Anyone can be a reformer, but it's quite another thing to reform.

❖ When some people pass the buck, they try to add the sales tax.

❖ He's the sort of chap who follows you into a revolving door and comes out first. – *William Hickey*

❖ People who sponge their way through life seldom wipe out their obligations.

❖ Don't argue with a woman—or a man. – *K-Lens-M Komments*

❖ Folks who live double lives find that neither is to be commended.

❖ Some of us veer to the left and some of us swing to the right, but most of us are self-centered. – *K-Lens-M Komments*

❖ Some people are like blotters—they soak it all in and get it all backwards. – *Hudson Newsletter*

❖ A pessimist had the following put on his tombstone: "I expected this and here I am."

❖ Gossips are people who tell you something, forget which one did the talking, and tell others you said it.

❖ Opportunists are those who play up what little they know to the greatest advantage.

❖ Some people never get interested in anything until it is none of their business.

❖ A bore talks mostly in the first person, a gossip in the third, and a brilliant conversationalist in the second. – *Boston Globe*

❖ People who no longer can grapple with a situation are on the verge of losing their grip.

❖ No power on earth can keep a first-class man down, or a fourth-class man up.

❖ A psychiatrist is sometimes referred to as a mind sweeper.

❖ It's easy to love your neighbor as yourself if she's pretty.

❖ It's hard for some people to heed the call of duty as long as there is something else worth listening to.

❖ A gossip usually gets caught in his own mouth-trap.

❖ People, like athletic teams, are never licked until they begin to complain about the rules of the game.

❖ People who jump at conclusions spend lots of time in the air.

❖ Most rumors come up the heard way. – *K-Lens-M Komments*

❖ One who is up and doing is never down and out.

❖ About the time you get even with the Joneses, they refinance.

❖ People who live busy lives never find time for hysterics.

❖ The best time to study human nature is when nobody else is present. – *Tom Masson*

Surprising Facts by K-Lens-M Komments

✓ A murderer's chances of being caught are 95 out of 100. (May, 1963)
✓ One out of five in the U. S. move each year. (May, 1963)

Procrastination

❖ Never put off until tomorrow the bad habit you can cut out altogether.

❖ Postponing a responsibility is decorating the rave of a good intention.

❖ When day is done, too many times we find out that not much else is.

❖ If you want to make an easy job seem mighty hard, just keep putting off doing it. – *Olin Miller, Chicago Sun-Times Syndicate*

❖ If it took an effort to go from today to tomorrow, some fellows would still be in yesterday.

❖ Procrastination is a fault that most people put off trying to correct. – *Indianapolis News*

❖ The seasons slip by and, before you know it, it's time for the bulbs you didn't get planted last fall not to come up.
– *Changing Times, The Kiplinger Magazine*

❖ No need to put your best foot forward if you drag the other one.

❖ It's a pretty safe bet that today's work put off until tomorrow, got the same treatment yesterday.

❖ If you figure you are going to do better tomorrow, why not start today?

❖ Turn your back to one problem and you'll come face to face with a dozen others.

❖ Always put off until tomorrow what you shouldn't do at all.

Responsibility

❖ It is easy to dodge responsibility, but you can't dodge the consequences of doing so.

❖ When you are contemplating revenge, it is well to remember that every other line of work pays better.

❖ If you should kick the person who is responsible for most of your troubles, you wouldn't be able to sit down for a month.

❖ Run from your responsibilities and you'll never go very far.

❖ Those who continue to shrink from responsibility, continue to shrink.

❖ Responsibilities: anchors of life. – *K-Lens-M Komments*

Revenge

❖ When you start to get even, why not get even with the man who has done you a favor?

❖ Sometimes folks do odd things to get even.

❖ No man can cash in on the satisfaction he gets out of revenge.

❖ If thine enemy wrong thee, buy each one of his children a drum.

❖ It costs much more to avenge a wrong than it does to let it go by default.

Science

- Naturally there is a lot of confusion about outer space, since the only people who really understand it are about ten years old and busy with school, Cub Scouts and piano lessons. – *Bill Vaughan*

- You don't need a telescope these days when looking for trouble. – *K-Lens-M Komments*

- Some day one is going to invent a mirror that is willing to lie, and he is going to make a fortune.

- Typical of a man's genius is the way he develops a bomb designed to drive us into the cellar about the time he starts building homes without any cellars. – *Homer King*

- The best way to get a man on the moon is to put a woman there first. – *K-Lens-M Komments* (October, 1965)

- Nowadays the college student who constantly stares into space is likely to get an engineering scholarship.

- Some of us don't know what we want, but feel sure we don't have it.

- Wernher von Braun: Sir Launch-a-lot – *Jack H. Maxwell*

- Why are we so anxious to conquer outer space when we haven't even solved the parking problem?

- Astronomers claim there is no sign of intelligent life on Mars.

There's little indication of it here, either. – *K-Lens-M Komments*

❖ Since I do not foresee that atomic energy is to be a great boon for a long time, I have to say that for the present it is a menace. Perhaps it is well that it should be. It may intimidate the human race into bringing order to its international affairs, which without the pressure of fear, it would not do. – *Albert Einstein*

❖ Whenever science makes a discovery, the devil grabs it while the angels are debating the best way to use it. – *Alan Valentine*

❖ Astronomers know more about the universe than the medical men know about the common cold.

❖ Thomas A. Edison was the man who invented the phonograph to keep us awake so that we would stay up all night using his electric light.

❖ There is much talk about H-bombs, but we hope the subject is never dropped.

❖ Naturalists who claim America's wild life is disappearing, don't stay up very late at night. – *K-Lens-M Komments* (October, 1965)

❖ After they conquer space, maybe we can get them to work on our parking problem.

❖ One of the first things a boy learns with a chemistry set is that he isn't likely ever to get another one. – *Don Revello*

❖ Mid planets and satellites tho' we may roam, be it ever so jumbled there's no space like home. – *K-Lens-M Komments* (April, 1964)

❖ As one little electron said to another when they met in a new element: "I don't know you from atom."

❖ Science has added years to our lives. All we need now is to find out how to add life to our years.

❖ The chemical components of the human body are worth $34.59. When this hits fifty bucks, we'll sell! – *K-Lens-M Komments* (March, 1964)

❖ The stars are not so strange as the mind that studies them, analyzes their light and measures their distance.
– *Harry Emerson Fosdick*

❖ People all over the world are beginning to wonder if splitting the atom was a wise crack.

❖ This space age taxes the imagination, too. – *K-Lens-M Komments* (April, 1964)

❖ Our two greatest problems are gravity and paper work. We can lick gravity, but sometimes the paper work is overwhelming.
– *Dr. Wernher von Braun, on the nation's space program*

❖ So far, science has not figured out how to tell what some people are thinking by what they are saying.

❖ One way to reach the moon would be to put all Sunday papers in one pile. – *K-Lens-M Komments* (May, 1963)

❖ Once upon a time when you said your battery was dead, you meant your car—not your toothbrush!
– *Changing Times, The Kiplinger Magazine*

❖ What this country needs is a medium-priced power mower that can be operated from an air-conditioned room.

❖ One thing about the speed of light is that it gets up too early in the morning.

❖ The only things left for science to control are women and the weather. – *K–Lens–M Komments*

Surprising Facts by **K-Lens-M Komments**

✓ A carat is one-fifth of a gram. (May, 1963)
✓ The U.S. buys half of the world's gem diamonds. (May, 1963)
✓ 24-carat gold is pure gold. (May, 1963)
✓ Rubies are extremely hard. (May, 1963)
✓ Diamonds are 90 times harder than the next hardest gem. (May, 1963)
✓ Pearls come from shellfish. (May, 1963)
✓ Some alloys weigh less than the average weight of the metals in them. (March, 1964)
✓ Heat makes air lighter. (May, 1964)
✓ Fog is a ground-level cloud. (May, 1964)
✓ Most U.S. winds are westerly. (May, 1964)
✓ Hailstones have killed people. (May, 1964)
✓ It is never too cold to snow. (May, 1964)
✓ After 93,000,000 miles to get to the earth, the sun's rays can burn badly in 15 minutes. (August, 1964)
✓ Water has an elastic surface film. (August, 1964)
✓ About 75 percent of the earth's surface is covered with water. (August, 1964)
✓ Seawater contains bromine. (August, 1964)
✓ Air is the most vital essential for human life. (August, 1964)
✓ About two-thirds of U.S. rainfall is on the eastern half. (August, 1964)
✓ A gallon of water weighs 8.4 pounds. (August, 1964)
✓ The average man takes in about a ton of water a year. (August, 1964)
✓ The U.S. averages more than 200 tornadoes a year. (August, 1965)
✓ Tornado winds reach 500 m.p.h. (August, 1965)
✓ Tornadoes revolve counterclockwise. (August, 1965)
✓ None of the U.S. is immune to tornadoes. (August, 1965)
✓ May and June are peak tornado months. (August, 1965)
✓ Most tornadoes occur between the hours of 3 and 7 p.m.

(August, 1965)
✓ The average width of the path of a tornado is 400 yards. (August, 1965)
✓ Tornadoes very seldom hit mountainous regions. (August, 1965)

Success & Determination

❖ Luck is the crossroad where planning and opportunity meet.

❖ 'Tis a wise man who can find a sensible answer to a foolish question.

❖ Taking things as they come and being able to live with them is another form of success.

❖ He who tries to please everybody shows little respect for his own thinking.

❖ The only way to get up in the world is to get down to serious business.

❖ Confucius say, "No man who catches large fish goes home through alley."

❖ Luck has been described as something that enables another person to succeed where we have failed.

❖ Don't blame any man for his poor start in life. It's the finish that he's responsible for.

❖ Real popularity is priceless; the kind you buy is worthless.

❖ Many so-called golden opportunities are only plated.

❖ What makes a contest so uneven is that certain people have brains and are willing to work hard.

❖ A good financier is a man whose wife never finds out when he gets a raise in salary.

❖ Experience is what causes people to make new mistakes instead of the same old ones.

❖ Sometimes you find a man who hasn't time to take advice—he's too busy selling it.

❖ Obstinacy is the strength of the weak.

❖ Trouble that looks like a mountain in the distance is frequently only a hill when you get to it.

❖ A great many people who don't know where they are going keep wondering why they don't get there.

❖ Success in any line means work. Nature freezes the water, but you are expected to cut your own ice.

❖ Good luck has to be met halfway; bad luck chases you.

❖ Some have tried and not succeeded, but no one has ever succeeded and not tried.

❖ People who have never failed can never appreciate success.

❖ We all have something to fall back on and I never knew a phony who didn't land on it eventually. – *Wilson Mizner*

❖ There will always be plenty of room at the top, but a man must be well balanced to stay there.

❖ Nothing is impossible to the man who does not have to do it himself. – *Earl Wilson*

❖ Some people never accomplish anything because they refuse to do a little at a time.

❖ The successful man is the one who does what he has to do at the time he hates to do it most.

❖ Too many people expect free passes on the road to success.

❖ To hear some people tell it, you'd think they deserved credit for the success of their ancestors.

❖ A hen is the only creature that can go on a sit-down strike and still produce results.

❖ The over-cautious man hesitates to put his best foot forward for fear of stubbing his toe.

❖ You can't acquire people's confidence by knocking.

❖ Worse than a quitter is a man who is afraid to begin.

❖ Plan your every move. The only difference between a mob and an army is organization.

❖ Lay the foundation for tomorrow's success today.

❖ A man can do more than he thinks he can, but usually less than he thinks he does. – *John M. Henry*

❖ A man cannot learn the ropes without falling on them a few times.

❖ You know a man is successful when the newspapers start quoting him on subjects he knows nothing about. – *Observer*

❖ One of the biggest troubles with success is that its recipe is often the same as that for a nervous breakdown.

❖ Over estimate your ability and you'll sometimes lose; under estimate your ability and you'll never even start.

❖ Tact is the art of getting what you want without letting the other fellow know you want it.

❖ Some people have ability and some have ambition; but those who succeed have both.

❖ Sometimes a fellow pins his faith to a star, and discovers later that it was only a firefly.

❖ Go as far as you can see; when you get there you'll see farther.

❖ Many a man and his good intentions go broke together.

❖ Don't worry if your dreams don't come true. Neither do your nightmares.

❖ One way to cover a bad past is to build a splendid future over it.

❖ The man who rolls up his sleeves seldom loses his shirt.

❖ The average man is as close to the top as to the bottom.

❖ The people who get the most kick out of life are those who kick the least.

❖ Don't try to find a man willing to hold the ladder while you climb to success.

❖ Days are like suitcases; all nearly the same size, but some people can pack a lot more into one.

❖ The self-made man will be treated with a great deal more respect when he equips himself with a silencer.

❖ Even though we may have an excellent aim in life, poor ammunition can cause many failures.

❖ The only difference between a stumbling block and a stepping stone is how high you lift your feet.

❖ Envy is a pain of mind that successful men cause their neighbors.

❖ The greatest trouble with luck is that it generally deserts you when you need it most.

❖ There is no limit as to how high a person can climb, but it is always necessary to start from the ground level.

❖ The dictionary is the only place where success comes before work. – *Bennet Cert*

❖ You cannot always pick winners, but it's easy to spot the man who is a loser.

❖ There is plenty of room at the bottom for those who lack the ambition to climb.

❖ Most people get what they deserve, but only the successful admit it.

❖ Many a man burns his fingers in his haste to strike while the iron is hot.

❖ Why praise a man who keeps both feet on the ground? He isn't getting anywhere.

❖ Progress involves risk. You can't steal second base and keep your foot on first.

❖ If you can convince yourself you are one of the chosen few, you will live to find out you are one of the disappointed many.

❖ Success is the world's rewards for many little things well done.

❖ You cannot get up in the world by throwing stones at those who have reached the top.

❖ When opportunity looks you over and then overlooks you, only you can be blamed.

❖ Tact consists in knowing how far to go too far. – *Jean Cocteau*

❖ Tact is the ability to let the other fellow have your way.

❖ He who pushes ahead by going back on his friends is lonely in his success.

❖ You're on the road to success when you realize that failure is merely a detour. – *William G. Milnes, Jr.*

❖ The enemy of the best is not the worst, but the good enough. – *L. P. Jacks*

❖ Never give a man up until he has failed at something he likes. – *Lewis E. Lawes*

❖ Things come to those who wait, but only the things left by those who hustle. – *Leo Aikman in Atlanta Constitution*

Timeless Teachings from Mrs. Stroupe's Blackboard

- ❖ It is surprising how little it takes to encourage ambitious men.

- ❖ Anyone can make some sort of a start in life, but it takes a good engineer to get anywhere.

- ❖ Most people would succeed in small things if they were not troubled with great ambitions.

- ❖ The world admits you have ability only after you have reached the top.

- ❖ Big men become big by doing what they didn't want to when they didn't want to.

- ❖ A game of chance is one in which you haven't got much chance.

- ❖ No man has ever been able to prove the excellence of his talents by shooting his critics.

- ❖ Some people stand around waiting for an opportunity that's already there. – *K-Lens-M Komments* (June, 1962)

- ❖ The world will always push a man along the road he has positively decided to follow.

- ❖ He who does nothing but wait for his ship to come in has already missed the boat.

- ❖ Strive always to be a winner and you'll never find fault with the referee's decision.

- ❖ Success in dealing with other people is like making rhubarb pie—use all the sugar you can, and then double it. – *Banking*

- ❖ A quitter never wins; a winner never quits.

❖ If you've made up your mind that you can't do something, you're absolutely right. – *The American Salesman*

❖ He who is unwilling to sweat for success is usually ready to swat those who have earned it.

❖ Better to have aimed high and missed than to have never aimed at all.

❖ An opportunist is a guy who is always able to land on somebody else's feet. – *Earl Wilson*

❖ Drift with the tide and eventually land on the rocks.

❖ Too many people think that luck is against them just because they have to work for what they get.

❖ A habit cannot be tossed out the window; it must be coaxed down the stairs a step at a time. – *Mark Twain*

❖ There's no limit to the good a man can do if he doesn't care who gets the credit.

❖ Triumph—adding umph to try. – *Arkansas Valley Farmer*

❖ The road to success is strewn with the bones of others' failures.

❖ Trouble falls on the just and unjust; and the unjust usually get to the umbrellas first.

❖ The fellow who works so hard to get to the front places himself in a good position to be kicked.

❖ If you have something to do that is worth doing, don't talk about it, but do it. After you have done it, your friends and enemies will talk about it.

❖ There are thousands of reasons for failure, but lack of advice is not one of them.

❖ It's the fellow who tries to do others who finds himself undone.

❖ About the only thing that comes to him who wants is wishes.

❖ You can't expect to win the game of life today with the hits you made yesterday.

❖ A man cannot be famous and successful if he isn't willing to pay the price.

❖ The orchestra leader got there by facing the music.

❖ Remember, the turtle has to stick his neck out to get anywhere.

❖ Punctuality is the art of being no later than anyone else.

❖ Any hill is too high for a poor climber.

❖ Whenever you think you can or you can't—you're right.

❖ If at first you don't succeed, you'll get a lot of unsolicited ideas and advice from those who didn't succeed, either.

❖ It isn't necessary to blow out the other fellow's light in order to let your own light shine.

❖ The only failure that really counts against a man's character is his failure to try.

❖ Too much talking and arriving nowhere is the same as climbing a tree to catch a fish.

❖ Think how much better the world would be if we were to let opportunity do all the knocking.

❖ A man never knows what he can do until he tries to undo what he has done. – *Frances Rodman*

❖ The best way to attain good luck is to watch for opportunities.

❖ An alarm clock won't make a man successful, it only reminds him of his opportunities.

❖ Fame is fleeting for the man who has a little success and tries to camp on it the rest of his life.

❖ Missing the boat is not nearly as bad as giving up the ship.

❖ Nothing is profitable which is dishonest.

❖ No venture can succeed as long as it remains only in your mind. Get busy.

❖ Every time the average person makes both ends meet, something breaks in the middle. – *Earl Wilson*

❖ A good start on the right road is only half the battle; a man must keep moving.

❖ A lost opportunity seems never able to find the way home.

❖ He who always does the best work is a success whether the world thinks so or not.

❖ Success is only a matter of luck; ask any man who failed.

❖ If you want to ride the train, you must get to the station before it leaves.

❖ Killing time is just another of many forms of success suicide.

❖ Too many Americans have the symbols without the status.
   – *K-Lens-M Komments*

❖ Opportunities travel on a one way street; once missed they never come back.

❖ Most of us think we are just as good as anybody else but unfortunately, our opinion doesn't prevail.

❖ A man who removes a mountain begins by carrying away small stones. – *Confucius*

❖ If you expect to be popular, you can't just do as you please.

❖ The simplest way to better your lot is to do a lot better.

❖ Reaching high keeps a man on his toes.

❖ A man may be the architect of his own fortunes, but he still can't get the sun in every room.

❖ A successful man is a combination of dollars and sense.

❖ If we want our dreams to come true, we must stay wide awake.

❖ The hardest thing about climbing the ladder of success is getting through the crowd at the bottom.

❖ Nothing wrong with having a high aim in life, but be sure the gun will carry to the target.

❖ He who plays both ends against the middle usually lands on the outside.

❖ No matter what your lot in life may be, build something on it.

❖ The man who dreams of past possibilities has a poor chance for success in the future.

❖ Honest men strive for the kind of success that needs no excuses.

❖ When a little success goes to a man's head, he's surely on the way to a head-on collision.

❖ A man's inclinations cause his downfall. – *K-Lens-M Komments*

❖ The man with an iron will is usually the first to rust out.

❖ Success is relative. The more success, the more relatives.

❖ The secret of success is to be forever pushing without seeming so.

❖ If you ever get the idea that you belong to the upper crust, just remember that the definition for upper crust is a lot of crumbs held together by a little dough.

❖ Things will come your way only when you decide to go after them.

❖ Keep on going and the chances are you will stumble on something, perhaps when you are least expecting it. I have never heard of anyone stumbling on something sitting down. – *Charles F. Kettering*

❖ You may overtake a lot of people on the road to ruin, but you never meet anyone returning.

❖ There are two kinds of failures: the man who will do nothing he is told, and the man who will do nothing.

❖ Lack of initiative causes a man to starve today while feeding on tomorrow's hopes.

❖ Some people go through life on their own initiative; others must be shoved across the line.

❖ The fellow who thinks he has the world by the tail often goes into a tailspin.

❖ Don't worry if you didn't land in a bed of roses. Just be thankful that your parachute opened.

❖ You can always tell luck from ability by its duration.

❖ One of our chief needs in life is somebody who will make us do what we can.

❖ On some self-made men, the building inspector must have been bribed. — *Independent Review*

❖ You can't carve your way to success by cutting remarks.

❖ Some complain about the noise whenever opportunity knocks. – *K-Lens-M Komments* (March, 1964)

❖ Only he who can see the invisible can do the impossible.

❖ The best way to make your dreams come true is to wake up. – *J. M. Power*

❖ Success comes to those who are too busy to look for it.

❖ Wisdom is knowing what to do next, skill is knowing how to do it, and virtue is doing it. – *David Starr Jordan, Everywoman's Family Circle*

❖ There is room at the top for you, but you must do your own climbing.

❖ I'd rather lose in a cause that will one day win than win in a cause that will someday lose. – *Woodrow Wilson*

❖ There is plenty of action in a rocking chair, but no progress.

❖ Men who never had to face failures seldom appreciate success.

❖ There are days when it seems that the black cat crossing our path must have had kittens. – *K-Lens-M Komments* (October, 1963)

❖ The underhanded means some people use to get ahead in this world could mean they are getting behind in the next.

❖ Calamities are of two kinds: misfortune to ourselves, and good fortune to others. – *Ambrose Bierce*

❖ Luck is what happens when preparation meets opportunity. – *Elmer G. Letterman*

❖ The big shots are only the little shots who keep shooting. – *Christopher Morley*

❖ It may be true that every man has his price, but a smart man never lets the price tag show.

❖ The straight and narrow has the lowest accident rate. – *K-Lens-M Komments*

❖ If at first you don't succeed, try a little ardor. – *Jack Waserman*

❖ Resourceful men do not pull great problems down to their level; they rise up and conquer them.

❖ He has what it takes who makes his own breaks. – *K-Lens-M Komments*

❖ It's usually the person with the winning hand who wants to put his cards on the table. – *Changing Times, The Kiplinger Magazine*

❖ Make the best of everything and you'll be guaranteed a market for your products.

❖ If you never stick your neck out, you'll never get your head above the crowd. – *Quoted in Wallaces' Farmer and Iowa Homestead*

❖ The main difference between a big shot and a little squirt is the noise they make.

❖ No matter how great a man is, the size of his funeral usually depends on the weather.

❖ Success and bad habits are seldom on speaking terms.

❖ A man owes it to himself to be successful. Once successful, he owes it to the Bureau of Internal Revenue.

❖ People who are convinced that this is a crooked old world should straighten their own course.

❖ Opportunity whistles as often as it knocks. – *K-Lens-M Komments* (May, 1965)

❖ I've one more resolution, and that's to stop making them—so I won't have to think up excuses for breaking them.

❖ Life is like a cafeteria. There are no waiters to bring success to you. You must help yourself.

❖ You get no place in a hurry when the only thing you're quick at is getting tired.

❖ Some people will never be accused of being quitters—they never start.

❖ The wheel of fortune loses its effectiveness when it turns a man's head.

❖ It's a lot easier to stop when you are climbing than when you are coming down.

❖ The will to win is seldom contested. – *K-Lens-M Komments*

❖ Luck is nothing but a tricky name for hard work.

❖ He who hesitates is last. – *Franklin P. Jones*

❖ Many of us spend half of our time wishing for things we could have if we didn't spend half our time wishing.

❖ He who hesitates is not only lost, he's miles from the next freeway exit. – *Leo J. Farrell, Jr.*

❖ The straight and narrow path will never be widened to carry the traffic.

❖ There's nothing wrong with the dreamer who gets up and hustles when the alarm clock rings.

❖ Many a self-made man has been known to suffer from remorse.

❖ Most of us don't get knocked down nearly as often as we lie down. – *K-Lens-M Komments* (August, 1964)

❖ The man who begins at the bottom never has very far to fall.

❖ It takes just as much energy to wish as it does to plan. – *Graphic*

❖ There's room at the top and bottom, but it's getting crowded in the middle. – *K-Lens-M Komments*

❖ It is impossible to get cornered on the straight and narrow path.

❖ Things may come to those to wait, but they are only the things passed up by those who hustle.

❖ We lay too much stress on stick-to-it-iveness. I once had a professor who wisely hung this sign over his desk: "Oh, Lord, teach me when to let go." – *W. G. Carleton*

❖ The man at the top wouldn't be where he is today if he hadn't been where he was yesterday.

❖ It's foolish to expect gains without pains. – *K-Lens-M Komments* (April, 1964)

❖ The young man who doesn't keep his eye on the clock but still knows what time it is will find unlimited opportunities in this growing country. – *William T. Noble*

❖ Even when opportunity knocks, a man has to get up off his seat to open the door.

❖ The man who has accomplished all that he thinks is worthwhile has begun to die.

❖ People who live in the past seem to think it is possible to back into success.

❖ If you aspire to the highest place, it is no disgrace to stop at the second, or even the third. – *Cicero*

❖ Opportunity knocks oftener than we answer. – *K-Lens-M Komments* (April, 1964)

❖ The reason some people can't turn over a new leaf is that the pages are all gummed up.

❖ Don't let yesterday use up too much of today. – *Will Rogers*

❖ Success: failure turned inside out. – *K-Lens-M Komments* (July, 1964)

❖ To stumble twice against the same stone is a disgrace.

❖ It is a rough road that leads to the heights of greatness.

❖ Chiselers never carve out successful careers.

❖ A critic is a legless man who teaches running.

Finally—Success

Failed in business '31
Defeated for Legislature '32
Again failed in business '33
Elected to Legislature '34
Sweetheart died '35
Had nervous breakdown '36
Defeated for Speaker '38
Defeated for Elector '40
Defeated for Land Officer '43
Defeated for Congress '43
Elected to Congress '46
Defeated for Congress '48
Defeated for Senate '55
Defeated for Vice-President '56
Defeated for Senate '58
Elected President 1860

Believe it or not, this is the record of Abraham Lincoln.

Temperament & Anger

- ❖ Temperamental: 2 percent mental and 98 percent temper.

- ❖ If you really are a live wire, people won't step on you.

- ❖ It's easy for a man to find a pretext for losing his temper, but there is never a good excuse.

- ❖ Anger is always worth less than it costs. – *K-Lens-M Komments* (October, 1965)

- ❖ The time to say nothing is when you feel like saying plenty.

- ❖ In many cases, the chip on a person's shoulder is just bark.

- ❖ One word leads to another, and eventually temper takes over.

- ❖ We love to overlook the boundaries that we do not wish to pass.

- ❖ The man with the fewest brains to spare is the most likely to lose his head.

- ❖ Tolerance is the ability to shrug your shoulder when you've got a chip on it.

- ❖ Nothing cooks a man's goose quicker than a red hot temper.

- ❖ When the other fellow acts that way, he's ugly; when you do, its nerves.

- ❖ Black eye: stamp of disapproval. – *K-Lens-M Komments*

❖ Anger improves nothing except the arch of a cat's back.
  – *Coleman Cox*

❖ A soft spot in one's heart is not to be confused with a soft spot in one's head.

❖ Anger is an acid that can do more harm to the vessel in which it is stored than to anything on which it is poured.

❖ A soft answer doesn't turn away a door-to-door salesman.
  – *K-Lens-M Komments* (June, 1962)

❖ The most destructive acid in the world is a sour disposition.

❖ Two occasions when the mouth should be shut: when chewing and when angry.

❖ Anger is a luxury few people can afford.

❖ The only reason why some men are found out of jail is because they have not been found out.

❖ The fellow with a fiery temper fills tomorrow with regrets.

❖ A sourpuss is made, not born. God gives us faces; we give ourselves expressions.

❖ He who boasts that he is levelheaded could never tell you at what level he leveled off.

❖ If you have a quick temper, don't think you are getting up in the world by hitting the ceiling.

❖ A chip on the shoulder simply adds useless weight to your burden.

❖ Anger makes your mouth work faster than your mind.

❖ A good trick if you can do it—keep your shirt on while getting a load off your chest.

❖ The more horse sense a man has, the less horsey he is.

❖ He who can prolong an argument until it wears itself out is usually a winner.

❖ Lack of stability discounts ability. – *K-Lens-M Komments*

❖ No crime is founded upon reason.

❖ Anger is one letter short of danger.

❖ Sometimes, when a man burns his bridges behind him, he finds that the road ahead is closed.

❖ Blackening a man's eyes is not the best way to enlighten him. – *K-Lens-M Komments* (September, 1963)

❖ The greatest remedy for anger is delay. – *Seneca*

❖ An argument proves only that at least two people are present.

❖ The fellow with an explosive temper often gets all banged up.

❖ It's hard for a fellow to keep a chip on his shoulder if you allow him to take a bow. – *Quoted by Billy Rose*

❖ In an argument, keep your words soft and sweet; you may be forced to eat them.

❖ Temper improves the more you don't use it. – *K-Lens-M Komments* (May, 1963)

❖ To have the last word is not what counts; having a word that lasts is what pays off.

❖ Two things a man should never be angry at: what he can help and what he cannot.

❖ Folks who go to pieces at the least provocation probably weren't put together right in the first place.

❖ When right, you can afford to keep your temper; when wrong, you can't afford to lose it.

❖ Arguments start most fights, but they never seem to finish one.

❖ People with hair-trigger tempers seem to lack a balance wheel.

❖ Once a man gets backed up against the wall, he'll have a hard time getting around it.

❖ Heated language has never been known to win a cold war.

❖ Far too many people will blow their top over anything or nothing. – *K-Lens-M Komments* (July, 1964)

❖ Some people are more even-tempered than others—they're mad all the time.

❖ Quarrels would not last long if the fault was only on one side.

❖ Keep your head and your temper. Only the small caliber man shoots off steam.

❖ Will power: the ability, after you have used three fourths of a can of paint and finished the job, to close the can and clean the brush, instead of painting something else that doesn't really need it. – *Indiana Telephone News*

Thoughtful Wisdom

❖ It often happens that the person who becomes lost in thought does so because he is in unfamiliar territory.

❖ The head never begins to swell until the mind stops growing.

❖ The intelligentsia are people who are ignorant of just how smart the ignorant people are.

❖ It may be quite true that ignorance is bliss, but there's a lot of bliss that isn't ignorance.

❖ A measure of a man's intelligence is his ability to discover when he is in the wrong.

❖ Science has never measured the capacity or incapacity of the human brain. – *K-Lens-M Komments* (October, 1965)

❖ There is always a bumper crop of food for thought, and not enough people to harvest it.

❖ Common sense is instinct. Enough of it is genius.
   – *George Bernard Shaw*

❖ It's all right to let your mind wander occasionally provided you don't try to follow it.

❖ The human capacity for being bored, rather than man's social or natural needs, lies at the root of man's cultural advance.
   – *Ralph Linton*

❖ Be exclusive if you wish, but at least stay on speaking terms with your conscience.

❖ A wise man carries his knowledge as he does his watch—not for display, but for his own use.

❖ Discussion: an argument that nobody is particularly interested in. – *Fletcher Knebel, The Register and Tribune Syndicate*

❖ Most of our troubles are caused by too much bone in the head and not enough in the back.

❖ To be wrong all the time is quite an effort, but some manage it.

❖ Some people look at ideas like they do at grandchildren; if they are their own, they are wonderful.

❖ Food for thought is the only kind that hasn't been affected by the high cost of living.

❖ Imagination is the eye of the mind. – *K-Lens-M Komments* (May, 1965)

❖ Weary minds are sooner refreshed by change than by idleness.

❖ Only the foolish and the dead never change their opinions.

❖ Knowledge is awareness of the fact that fire will burn; wisdom is remembrance of the blisters.

❖ The age of wisdom: when a man has a lot to say and doesn't say it.

❖ It is what you learn after you know it all that counts.

❖ Making up your mind is like making a bed; it usually helps to have someone on the other side. – *Gerald Horton Bath*

❖ It would take more than a hearing aid for some people to hear that low, small voice of conscience.

❖ People who don't know anything should keep it to themselves.

❖ If I do not believe as you believe, it proves that you do not believe as I believe, and this is all that it proves. – *Thomas Paine*

❖ A sure way to deceive yourself is to get the idea that you are smarter than the other fellow.

❖ What you don't know may not hurt you, but it certainly does amuse a lot of people.

❖ Scarcity of great leaders today, comparable to those reported in history, may indicate that people are beginning to do a little thinking for themselves.

❖ The measure of a man's intelligence is his ability to discover when he is in the wrong.

❖ Her train of thought was wrecked by a flood of emotion.

❖ Some people think all the equipment you need to discuss religion, politics or the mass transportation system is a mouth.

❖ Occasionally we meet a person whose brain might be defined as a scheme engine.

❖ A person who buries his head in the sand offers an engaging target. – *Mabel A. Keenan*

❖ You have a perfect right to your opinion—provided it agrees with mine.

❖ How pleasant it would be if one's memory could be like a sundial and record only the sunny hours.

❖ The easiest way to get into trouble is to be right at the wrong time.

❖ It's not hard to tell a wise man—he thinks that you are intelligent. – *K-Lens-M Komments* (October, 1963)

❖ Intelligence is a sterling quality possessed by anybody who will listen attentively to what you have to say and nod in agreement.

❖ Usually a dash of judgment is better than a flash of genius.

❖ A parachute is akin to one's mind. It works only when it is open.

❖ An expert is one who is just beginning to understand how little he knows about the subject.

❖ A closed mind is an enigma indeed. Nothing ever goes in—but odd things are forever coming out. – *Laurence Dunphy*

❖ Too often it's the budding genius who fails to bear good fruit.

❖ A handful of common sense is worth a bushel of learning.

❖ Nature seldom makes a fool. She merely furnishes the raw material for a do-it-yourself job.

❖ The stomach is the only part of a man that can be fully satisfied. The yearning of man's brain for new knowledge and experience and for more pleasant and comfortable surroundings never can be completely met. It is an appetite that cannot be appeased. – *Thomas A. Edison*

❖ We should make the same use of books that the bees do of the flowers; they gather sweets from them, but do not injure them.

❖ It is a single-track mind with no way to sidetrack prejudice that produces intolerance.

❖ Conscience is like gossip—few believe all they hear.
  – *K-Lens-M Komments* (March, 1964)

❖ Words are the dress of thoughts, which should never be presented in rags and tatters.

❖ Common sense is not so common.

❖ A great leader never permits his followers to discover that he is as dumb as they are.

❖ He knows the water best who has waded through it.

❖ We are not what we think we are, but what we think—we are.

❖ A wise man is like a tack; his head keeps him from going too far.

❖ Some people read just enough to keep themselves misinformed.

❖ Few minds wear out; more rust out.

❖ Life's greatest achievement is the continual remaking of yourself so that at last you know how to live.
  – *Smiley Blanton and Normal Vincent Peale*

❖ By confessing their ignorance, people place themselves in a position to learn.

❖ No one is too old to learn, but many people keep putting it off.

❖ They tell us that genius has its limits; stupidity, however, is not thus handicapped.

❖ Wisdom is knowing when to speak your mind and when to mind your speech.

❖ Some men don't seem to realize that they can learn a little every day and still not know it all.

❖ We must treat ideas somewhat as though they were baby fish. Throw thousands out into the water. Only a handful will survive—but that is plenty. – *Anne Heywood*

❖ It is easier to be wise for others than for ourselves. – *La Rochefoucauld*

❖ Great minds have purposes. Others have wishes. – *Washington Irving*

❖ A fellow with a bad memory is not necessarily he who forgets. He just happens to remember the wrong things.

❖ No brain is stronger than its weakest think.

❖ Self-seeking always warps judgment.

❖ An ignorant person is one who doesn't know anything about what you know, and knows things you didn't know anything about.

❖ Conscience: a thinking man's filter. – *The Liguorian*

❖ Great minds discuss ideas; normal minds discuss events; small minds discuss persons; until they shake down into classifications, they dwell on the possibility of rain tomorrow. — *News, Eunice, Louisiana*

❖ The best cosmetic in the world is an active mind that is always finding something new. – *Mary Meek Atkeson*

❖ Even good ideas won't last long unless they are put to work.

❖ Some folks who claim they can see both sides of a question are either up a tree or on a fence.

❖ Tact: getting your point across without stabbing someone with it. – *Richard Gordon in Boys' Life*

❖ Men are most apt to believe what they least understand.

❖ Nothing is wrong with the mind of a man who minds his own business.

❖ It is harder to conceal ignorance than to acquire knowledge. – *Arnold H. Glasgow in Quote*

❖ Think! It may be a new experience.

❖ If some people got a penny for their thoughts, they would be overpaid.

❖ You can't stop people from thinking, but you can start them.

❖ Conscience doesn't keep you from doing anything. It just keeps you from enjoying it.

❖ Most people think that a man won't listen to reason just because he does not agree with them.

❖ Some folks feel that their thinking is getting broader, but it is more likely that their conscience is stretching.

❖ The only time some folks think is when they think of themselves.
— *K-Lens-M Komments*

❖ There is a difference between good, sound reasons, and reasons that sound good.

❖ Ignorance ceases to be bliss to those seeking information.

❖ No horse gets anywhere until he is harnessed. No stream or gas ever drives anything until it is confined. No Niagara is ever turned into light and power until it is tunneled. No life ever grows great until it is focused, dedicated, disciplined.
— *Harry Emerson Fosdick*

❖ It doesn't require a high degree of intelligence to outsmart yourself.

❖ There is one thing to be said about ignorance—it sure causes a lot of interesting arguments. — *Harwell, Georgia, Sun*

❖ Books are lighthouses built on the sea of time. — *Whipple*

❖ Keep a clear conscience and you'll always be cool under fire.

❖ Philosophy is just common sense in a dress suit.

❖ The great difficulty with us all in our ignorance is to get to see our ignorance.

❖ Research is to see what everybody else has seen, and think what nobody has thought. — *Dr. Albert Szent-Györgyi, Science of Mind*

❖ Flights from reality cause many a man to make a crash landing.

❖ The deterrent to progress in the world is that 95 percent of the thinking is done by five percent of the people.

❖ The door to wisdom swings on the hinges of common sense and uncommon thoughts.

❖ Good judgment is founded on the true value of things—not on individual opinions of them.

❖ The larger the island of knowledge, the longer the shoreline of wonder. – *Ralph Sockman*

❖ Wisdom is merely an uncommon degree of common sense.

❖ Take time to figure out all the angles and you won't have to run around in circles.

❖ Ingenuity is man's cleverness in getting out of spots his stupidity got him into.

❖ A wise man isn't as sure of anything as a fool is sure of everything.

❖ Knowledge is the only thing that doesn't become secondhand when used.

❖ Streams of oratory do not always come from fountains of thought.

❖ There is no more terrible sight than ignorance in action. – *Goethe*

❖ The trouble with today's "herd thinking" is that too many of us think what we heard last. – *K-Lens-M Komments*

❖ Sometimes a clear conscience is nothing more than a poor memory.

❖ Bad luck often gets blamed, when lack of common sense should.

❖ Intuition is reason in a hurry. – *Holbrook Jackson*

❖ The most underdeveloped territory in the world lies under your hat.

❖ Wise are the folks who keep others from getting wise to them.

❖ Life is one long battle of wits—and think of all the brave folks who fight it unarmed. – *"Hector" in London News Chronicle*

❖ Those who remember the past with a clear conscience need have no fear of the future.

❖ The reason there are so few good talkers in public is that there are so few thinkers in private. – *Anonymous*

❖ Many a man who starts on a good idea fails because the idea wouldn't work unless he did.

❖ A good memory is one trained to forget the trivial.
   – *Clifton Fadiman*

❖ It's too bad more people are thoughtless than speechless.

❖ Reading is to the mind what exercise is to the body.
   – *Joseph Addison*

❖ Wisdom is in the head and not in the beard.

❖ Talk and the world talks with you; think and you think alone.
   – *K-Lens-M Komments* (May, 1964)

❖ You can wait for a train of thought, but don't depend on it arriving on time.

❖ The human mind doesn't need to be stuffed with information. It just needs to be open.

❖ Some people are intelligent enough to speak on any subject. Others don't need a subject.

❖ Historians tell us of the past; economists tell us of the future; but neither helps us much in the confused present.

❖ The ultimate sin of the mind is the failure to pay enough attention. – *John Ciardi*

❖ People wouldn't be running around in circles if they took time to study all the angles.

❖ Worry won't solve a problem; it only prevents a solution.

❖ Genius: concealed drudgery. – *K-Lens-M Komments*

❖ Only a genius can defy public opinion without being crushed.

❖ If the do-it-yourself craze continues, it might even extend to thinking.

❖ It wasn't until quite late in life that I discovered how easy it is to say, "I don't know." – *Somerset Maugham*

❖ There's nothing new under the sun—and the same old stuff is going on under the moon.

❖ Second thoughts are best only when they arrive on time.

❖ Conscience: the torture chamber of the soul. – *K-Lens-M Komments* (May, 1964)

❖ Your opinion is worthless unless you can get others to endorse it.

❖ It does a man no good to sit up and take notice—if he continues to sit.

❖ Too often a genius turns out to be a bird who can't even feather his own nest.

❖ The fool wanders, the wise man travels.

❖ Knowledge may be power; but it's amazing how many unsuccessful men know it all.

❖ Conscience: one witness you can't bribe. – *K-Lens-M Komments* (June, 1962)

❖ The past counts, but not so much as the todays and tomorrows.

❖ The test of a man is how well he is able to feel about what he thinks. The test of a woman is how well she is able to think about what she feels. – *Mary S. McDowell*

❖ A book isn't necessarily dry inside because there's dust on the outside.

❖ Don't become disturbed at anyone for knowing more than you do. It is really not his fault.

❖ Any good idea will work, but not unless you decide to work, too.

❖ It's easier to get folks to talk than to get them to think.

❖ Hunch: an idea you think may be wrong. – *K-Lens-M Komments* (September, 1963)

❖ People who think they know it all seldom demonstrate that knowledge is power.

❖ A little knowledge becomes a dangerous thing only when it

remains that size.

❖ Give some people a choice of two evils, and they'll take both.

❖ The thicker the skull, the sharper the hint must be to penetrate it.

❖ An intelligence test sometimes shows a man how smart he'd have been not to take it. – *G. Norman Collie*

❖ Light travels 1,000,000 times faster than sound, but not through the mind. – *K-Lens-M Komments* (May, 1963)

❖ Many a man has the capabilities of a genius, and not enough common sense to put them into practice.

❖ You can't any more explain what you don't know, than you can come back from where you haven't been.

❖ There are two ways to slide easily through life: to believe everything or to doubt everything. Both ways save us from thinking. – *Alfred Korzybski*

❖ If you're one who believes no two people think alike, look over a bride's wedding presents. – *K-Lens-M Komments* (June, 1962)

❖ Some men divide their time between trying to forget and trying to recover from the effects of trying to forget.

❖ It's too bad the fellow who gets carried away with his cleverness isn't.

❖ The ignorant tend to be distrustful of the informed; the informed, disdainful of the ignorant. Thus, some stumble in darkness while others are blinded by light. – *J. Ray Braswell*

❖ Wisdom is in knowing the difference between pulling your

weight and throwing it around.

❖ The world is shrinking faster than understanding expands.
 – *K-Lens-M Komments*

❖ Water on the brain has nothing to do with the thirst for knowledge.

❖ Don't be afraid to use your brain; it's the little things that count.

❖ Broad-minded people are those whom we can convince that our way of thinking is right.

Ten Things I Wish I Had Known Before I Was 21
1. That it was really important to be a Christian.
2. What I was going to do for a living—exactly what my life work would be.
3. That my health after 30 depended in a large degree on what I put into my stomach before I was 21.
4. How to take care of money—that I was really a trustee of what I had.
5. The asset of being neatly and sensibly dressed.
6. That habits are mighty hard to change after you're 21.
7. That worthwhile things require time, patience and work.
8. That the world would give me just about what I deserved.
9. That a thorough education not only pays better wages than hard labor, but it brings the best of everything else.
10. The value of absolute truthfulness in everything.
11. And one more for extra thought—That my parents weren't old fogies after all!

888888888888888888

Surprising Facts by K-Lens-M Komments

- ❖ Monotony slows creativity and imagination. (May, 1963)
- ❖ Dolphins may be the world's wisest creatures. An average-sized dolphin's brain weighs 3.5 lbs.—an average man's 3.1 – a chimpanzee's .75. (August, 1965)
- ❖ Psychologists say it's hard for the average person to remember more than seven items on a list. (October, 1965)

Time

❖ Many people are not satisfied to kill time unless it belongs to someone else.

❖ Attempting to leave footprints in the sands of time is the cause of many people getting stuck in the mud.

❖ Time is money, but it has no exchange value unless it is accompanied by hard work.

❖ The future is seldom as foreboding as it appears—the past always looks better than it was. – *K-Lens-M Komments* (May, 1965)

❖ The trouble with leaving footprints on the sands of time is proof that many people have traveled backward.

❖ This time, like all other times, is a very good one, if we but know what to do with it. – *Ralph Waldo Emerson*

❖ The full use of today is the best preparation for tomorrow.

❖ Sixty seconds make a minute. How much good can I do in it? – *A. U.*

❖ The main trouble with the future is that it keeps getting shorter and shorter.

❖ Time heals all things—except a leaky roof. – *K-Lens-M Komments* (August, 1963)

❖ Time may be money, but friends appreciate the money you spend on them more than the time spent.

❖ A person with an hour to kill usually spends it with someone who hasn't.

❖ He who brags the most about his future probably has a shady past he'd like to forget.

❖ Don't expect time to work for you if you try to kill it.
— *K-Lens-M Komments* (April, 1964)

❖ The morning hour has gold in its mouth.

❖ The easiest way to get into trouble is to be right at the wrong time!

❖ If you desire to leave footprints on the sands of time, start walking.

❖ The future and the past have a lot in common with the present.

❖ That extra hour of daylight assumes increased importance now that it is risky to venture out after dark. — *K-Lens-M Komments* (May, 1965)

❖ No one knows his best days until they are added to his past.

❖ Time is money, but don't spend a dollar's worth of time trying to save a penny.

❖ Time is money, but it can't be counterfeited. — *K-Lens-M Komments*

❖ By watching the clock, you cannot fail to learn that it passes the time by keeping its hands busy.

❖ The time a man turns in has a lot to do with the way he turns out.

311

❖ Today the future becomes the past almost before a man realizes it is present.

❖ Time is money—especially a good time. – *K-Lens-M Komments* (August, 1965)

❖ Time and money never go faster than when a person is on vacation.

Truth

❖ The trouble with stretching the truth is that it's apt to snap back.

❖ Most of our so-called reasoning consists of finding arguments for going on believing as we already do.

❖ A talebearer is a person who puts two and two together and makes a scandal of it.

❖ There wouldn't be much wrong with little white lies if the teller didn't sooner or later become color blind.

❖ Truth is polygonal. I never feel sure that I have got it until I have contradicted myself five or six times. – *John Ruskin*

❖ Dishonesty is never an accident.

❖ White lie: an attempt to color the truth. – *K-Lens-M Komments* (October, 1963)

❖ Truth does not do as much good in the world as its appearances do evil.

❖ The peak years of mental activity are undoubtedly between the ages of four and 18. At four, we know all the questions. At 18, we know all the answers.

❖ Honesty may be the best policy, but when some people tell the truth it is solely for the purpose of creating trouble.

❖ Truth may be bottled up, but eventually it pops the cork.

- It's not hard to find the truth; what is hard is not to run away from it once you have found it.

- History tells the truth about people after they are gone.

- A half-truth is the most cowardly of all lies. – *K-Lens-M Komments* (March, 1964)

- As great as truth is, the supply is always greater than the demand. – *Josh Billings*

- Keeping a secret from some people is like trying to smuggle daylight past a rooster.

- Truth is the highest thing a man can keep. – *Chaucer*

- Excuse: stallibi. – *K-Lens-M Komments* (July, 1964)

- Arguments always ensue when ten people try to keep each other from finding out the truth.

- It seems that the only thing new under the sun are the methods used in distorting the truth.

- Most excuses are little white lies wrapped in cellophane.

- Be truthful and lose temporarily or lie and lose permanently.

- A lie has short legs, truth overtakes it.

- When in doubt what to say, why not take a chance of getting by with the truth?

- A liar can always get another liar to swear he's telling the truth.

- People who beat around the bush take the long road to nowhere.

Truth

❖ Letting the cat out of the bag is much easier than putting it back.

❖ Not only do falsehoods disagree with truths, but they usually quarrel amongst themselves.

❖ Truth is stranger than fiction—you don't encounter it as often.
 – *K–Lens–M Komments* (August, 1964)

❖ The truth doesn't hurt until it ought to.

❖ Better to suffer for the truth than be rewarded for a lie.

❖ The truth hurts—and so would anything else that was stretched that much.

❖ There are two sides to every story, and some people can improvise several more.

Vacation & Adventure

❖ A tourist is a man who travels to see things that are different and then complains when they aren't the same. – *Dublin Opinion*

❖ It's when you're safe at home that you wish you were having an adventure. When you're having an adventure, you wish you were safe at home. – *Thornton Wilder*

❖ Vacation is a period during which people find out where to stay away from next year.

❖ Leisure is a beautiful garment, but it will not do for constant wear.

❖ A souvenir is a far-fetched reminder. – *K-Lens-M Komments* (October, 1965)

❖ The bigger the summer vacation, the harder the fall. – *Somerset, P.A., American*

❖ Hotel: a place where a guest often gives up good dollars for poor quarters.

❖ Summer tourists: people who will put up with any inconvenience in search for all the comforts of home. – *Fletcher Knebel*

❖ When some careless campers are through with the scenery they burn it. – *K-Lens-M Komments* (August, 1964)

❖ The rainy day for which we save our money generally arrives at vacation time.

❖ If the designers of women's bathing suits aren't careful, they'll soon be out of a job! – *Sheraton-Park Hotel News*

❖ You can usually tell the guy who's just returned from vacation; he's the one who looks as though he needs one. – *Earl Wilson*

❖ Adventure: discomfort seen at a distance. – *Edward Ellis*

❖ Home: the place where the college student home for vacation isn't. – *Evan Esar*

❖ Geyser: inverted waterfall. – *K-Lens-M Komments* (April, 1964)

❖ Pleasures from vacation trips may not exceed expectations— but expenses always do.

❖ Vacation's end: when dispositions, the shore and the lawn all become crabby. – *Marcelene Cox*

❖ Why doesn't work vacation when you do? – *K-Lens-M Komments*

❖ Young thing at the beach: "Darn! I left my suit in my other wallet!" – *Dick Turner*

❖ A vacation usually consists of 2 weeks, which are 2 short. Then you are 2 tired 2 return 2 work and 2 broken not 2. 2 bad!

❖ A pocketbook is a depressed area after a vacation trip.

❖ Everyone should travel—if only to get themselves better acquainted with the comforts of home.

❖ About the only thing that moves faster than the speed of sound is a two weeks' vacation.

❖ The vacation that's most glad and gay is enjoyed when the boss is away. – *K–Lens–M Komments* (August, 1964)

❖ One returned tourist reports the satisfactory completion of his trip—he beat all his checks home. – *Bill Vaughan*

❖ Nowadays, a travel folder is referred to as a trip tease.

❖ It is hard to understand a person who travels many miles to admire the scenery, then litters it with garbage.

❖ If all the boarders in all the boarding houses were placed side by side at a table, they would still reach.

❖ Our travel pictures prove that we saw many foreign spots, but how I wish that we concurred on where we took the shots! – *Lenore Eversole Fisher*

❖ An upper birth is where you rise to retire and get down to get up.

❖ A gal has her choice: go to the mountains and see the scenery or go to the beach and be the scenery. – *Hal Cochran*

❖ Summer resort: seasonal strutting ground where nobody knows how unimportant you are at home.

❖ Despite jets, missiles and such, nothing goes faster than a two-week vacation. – *Earl Wilson*

❖ Bathing suit: garment cut down to see level. – *K–Lens–M Komments* (April, 1964)

❖ A vacation is what some people take when they can't take what they have been taking any longer.

❖ We take vacation trips to relax, but after returning home we can't feel any change.

❖ Recreation: getting exhausted on your own time. – *K-Lens-M Komments* (August, 1963)

❖ A sure way to get a bang out of a vacation is to take a detour on thin tires.

❖ A vacation is a short duration of recreation, preceded by a period of anticipation, and followed by a period of recuperation.

❖ People go on vacation to forget things and when they open their grips find out they did. – *Hal Cochran*

❖ The really happy man is the one who can enjoy the scenery when he has to take a detour. – The Wall Street Journal

❖ Some who vacation to forget everything, take everything along. – *K-Lens-M Komments* (July, 1964)

❖ Vacation: three weeks on the sands—the rest of the year on the rocks. – *Cedric Adams*

Women

- The only way to understand any woman is to love her—and then it isn't necessary to understand her. – *Sydney J. Harris*

- The best thing about women is that there's so many of them.

- A man is as old as he feels, and a woman is as old as she feels like admitting.

- Many an old maid feels that the world owes her a loving.

- When a woman meets a man who looks her straight in the eye, she'd better do something about her figure.

- It isn't logical for women to be logical. – *K-Lens-M Komments* (May, 1965)

- When a pretty woman joins the police force, she immediately arrests attention.

- Girls are what women over forty-five call each other.

- Thirty is a nice age for a woman—especially if she happens to be fifty.

- There are two kinds of women: the fashionable ones and those who are comfortable.

- She says her photographs don't do her justice, but she doesn't really want justice—she wants mercy. – *The Safe Worker*

❖ Women have a tougher time than a public accountant keeping their figures straight.

❖ Asking a woman her age is just like buying a secondhand car. You know the speedometer has been turned back, but you haven't any idea as to how far.

❖ Women like to look on the bride side.

❖ Some of the new spring millinery could be called ridiculous on the sublime. – *K-Lens-M Komments* (March, 1964)

❖ A certain woman we know is an excellent housekeeper. Every time she gets a divorce she keeps the house.

❖ Are women who say they have nothing to wear, dresstitute?

❖ If a girl doesn't watch her figure, the boys won't.

❖ Women were made before mirrors … and they've stayed there ever since!

❖ It would seem that some women get their hairstyles by watching birds build their nests.

❖ Gals who are active are far more attractive. – *K-Lens-M Komments* (October, 1963)

❖ Some people aren't so good at counting calories and have the figures to prove it.

❖ Doing a woman's work is like walking down a railroad track: the end seems in sight but never is. – *Marcelene Cox*

❖ Intuition is that strange instinct that tells a woman she is right, whether she is or not.

❖ A woman who looks like a dumb blonde might really be a bright brunette.

❖ Woman: an illogical creature who uses her intelligence to find reasons to support her intuition. – *General Features Corp*

❖ Padded girdle: stern unreality. – *K-Lens-M Komments* (May, 1965)

❖ The only slim thing about her figure is her chance of getting it back. – *Glen Preston Burns*

❖ They say there are several ways to handle a woman. What a shame that no one knows what they are.

❖ A low neckline is about the only thing a man will approve of and look down on at the same time.

❖ By the time a man understands women, he is no longer interested.

❖ When a woman refuses to tell you her weight, you can be sure she weights a hundred and plenty.

❖ Fashions that are wearable most women find unbearable. – *K-Lens-M Komments* (May, 1965)

❖ She even has a nagging cough. – *Myron Scarbrough*

❖ When it comes to spreading gossip, the female of the species is much faster than the mail. – *Houghton Line*

❖ One reason why girls kiss and make up is that the stuff rubs off. – *Paris Pups*

❖ If women dress to please men, why does it take 'em so long?

❖ Nine gals out of ten can't whistle or wink, but they get by much better than you'd think. – *K-Lens-M Komments*

❖ Just about the time you try to teach your children that you can't put more into a container than it can hold, along comes a woman wearing slacks.

❖ Since the discovery of elastic, it is estimated women take up one-third less space.

❖ If women are not dangerous, why do men always increase their insurance when they marry?

❖ A girl who looks like a million dollars shouldn't walk like loose change.

❖ There are four things a woman needs to know. She needs to know how to look like a girl, act like a lady, think like a man, and work like a dog. – *Mrs. Caroline K. Simon*

❖ Women can talk themselves out of anything except a phone booth. – *K-Lens-M Komments*

❖ A woman who says she couldn't care less means she couldn't care more.

❖ When a woman reaches her 40th birthday, it's just like launching a rocket. That's when they start the countdown.

❖ Changeable women are more endurable than monotonous ones. They are sometimes murdered, but seldom deserted. – *George Bernard Shaw*

❖ Nothing is harder on a woman's clothes than another woman.

❖ Then there was the blonde who said she would be happy as long as she could keep her hair light and her past dark.

❖ A lady is a woman who makes it easy for a man to be a gentleman.

❖ To put her in a rage, just ask her weight or age. – *K-Lens-M Komments*

❖ Feminine logic is fallacious, shallow, inconsistent, irrelevant, capricious, transparent—and irrefutable. – *Harold Coffin*

❖ The new dress a woman buys has to be just like everybody else's, but not like anybody else's. – *Harold Coffin*

❖ If a gal can remember that figures don't lie, it's a lot easier to stick to a diet.

❖ Faint complexion never won fair husband. – *K-Lens-M Komments* (May, 1965)

❖ Never argue with a woman when she's tired—or rested. – *H. C. Diefenbach in P-K Sideliner*

❖ There's no effective defense against a hydrogen blonde attack, either. – *K-Lens-M Komments* (April, 1964)

❖ What this country needs is a lady's shoe that is larger on the inside than on the outside. – *Maureen Coper*

❖ The perfect gift for the girl who has everything is penicillin. – *Mrs. B. Harris*

❖ Never underestimate the purr of a woman. – *Toronto Daily Star*

❖ A new hat is not only a tonic for a woman, but it makes her feel

strong enough to buy a suit and four pairs of shoes to go with it.
– *Herbert V. Prochnow*

❖ She spent her afternoon at the beauty shop getting curled to strike. – *Henrietta Plate*

❖ A chance remark is anything a man manages to say when two women are talking.

❖ Women's hats are different because no one likes to make the same mistakes twice.

❖ A youthful figure is something you get when you ask any woman her age.

❖ Hollywood crack: "She's old enough to be his wife." – *Earl Wilson*

❖ A girl's biggest asset is a man's imagination.

❖ Artist's model: a girl unsuited for her work. – *Phoenix Flame*

❖ Bridge: a game that gives women something to try to think about while they are talking. – *General Features Corp.*

❖ You know her—she goes through life with her horn stuck. – *Mignon McLaughlin*

❖ Sympathy: what one girl offers another in exchange for details.

❖ Bikinis show a gal off or show her up. – *K-Lens-M Komments* (August, 1965)

❖ In dress shop: "But, madam, looking ridiculous is the fashion this summer!" – *Mike Connolly*

❖ There are eight reasons why a woman buys something: because her husband says she can't have it, it will make her look thin, it comes from Paris, the neighbors can't afford it, nobody has one, everybody has one, it's different, and *because.* – *Mrs. E. L. R. in True Story Magazine*

❖ Gals least talkative are most provocative. – *K-Lens-M Komments* (May, 1965)

❖ You never can tell about women; even if you can, you shouldn't.

❖ Those who have no trouble separating the men from the boys are commonly called women.

❖ What every woman wants is more.

❖ Few women are so scatterbrained they can't pay clothes attention. – *K-Lens-M Komments*

❖ Woman: a person who stands 20 minutes talking at a door because she hasn't time to come in.

❖ Becoming plump is routine for a woman; she just fills out a form. – *Earl Wilson*

❖ Getting a word in edgewise with some women is like threading a sewing machine with the motor running. – *Pic Larmour*

❖ Many women could add years on their lives by telling the truth.

❖ That famed intuition, the feminine hunch, never tells what a husband is having for lunch. – *Margaret Evelyn Singleton*

❖ Secret: something a woman can keep with a telling effect. – *Paul H. Gilbert*

❖ Women give more time to beauty than education because no

matter how stupid a man may be, he isn't blind.

❖ Cigars are more jealous than women. If they feel you're losing interest in them, they stop burning! – *Arthur Rubinstein*

❖ Just about the time a woman thinks her work is done, she becomes a grandmother. – *Edward H. Dreschnack*

❖ These new stockings made of coal, wood, and rubber could be very confusing for women. When they get a run, they don't know whether they have a clinker, a splinter, or a blowout.

❖ If a girl doesn't try to hold her shape, no one else will, either. – *D. O. Flynn*

❖ A tomboy is a girl who hasn't yet discovered that her strength lies in her weakness. – *Eldon Pedersen*

❖ The most curious thing in the world is a woman who isn't. – *Advocate, Amherst, Wisconsin.*

❖ Charge: the final word in women's fashions. – *E. K. Banfill*

❖ Whatever happened to that wonderful type of woman who couldn't stand a man underfoot when she was doing housework? – *General Features Corp.*

❖ Cosmetics are a woman's way of keeping a man from reading between the lines. – *Dan Bennett*

❖ When a woman suffers in silence, it probably means her phone is out of order. – *Tom Sims*

❖ Two women saying goodbye: much ado about nothing. – *Gaston Citizen*

❖ Some blondes never fade—they just dye away. – *Ann Landers*

❖ Any man who says he can see through women is missing a lot. – *Harold Coffin*

❖ Pedal pushers: a kind of pants worn as a compromise by a woman whose husband can't decide whether she looks worse in slacks or Bermuda shorts.

❖ Girl: a person who will scream at a mouse but smile at a wolf. – *Phil Stone in Toronto Telegram*

❖ At a bargain sale, a woman can ruin one dress while she buys another.

❖ Bathing beauty: a girl worth wading for. – *General Features Corp.*

❖ What a lot of women would like to do with last year's dress is get into it. – *Anthony J. Pettito*

❖ A miss is as good as her guile. – *K-Lens-M Komments*

❖ Modern paintings are like women. You'll never enjoy them if you try to understand them. – *Harold Coffin*

❖ A woman's final decision is not necessarily the same as the one she makes later. – *H. N. Ferguson*

❖ When a woman yields to logic, she probably has a good reason of her own, too. – *Franklin P. Jones*

❖ A woman's promise to be on time carries a lot of wait. – *Mimi Kurtz*

❖ We are a generation that seems about to give up the use of legs.

Women are the only ones smart enough to find a use for them.
– *Dr. Irvine H. Page, NEA*

❖ Women do things for appearance for which used-car dealers would go to jail. – *Robert Yoder*

❖ Counter-irritant: a woman who shops all day and doesn't buy anything. – *Wilcox Antenna*

❖ Anyone who thinks chemical warfare is new doesn't know much about perfume.

❖ American women spend a billion a year on beauty. That's why so many of 'em look like a million! – *K-Lens-M Komments* (May, 1964)

❖ The reason the average girl would rather have beauty than brains is that the average man can see better than he can think.

❖ By looking into any woman's pocketbook, one discovers that money isn't everything. – *Changing Times, The Kiplinger Magazine*

❖ When a girl finds she's not the only pebble on the beach, she usually becomes a little bolder. – *Columbus Ohio State Journal*

❖ It's not clothes that make men stare—it's what isn't there. – *K-Lens-M Komments* (May, 1963)

❖ A doctor can't persuade a woman to go on a diet half as fast as last year's bathing suit can. – *Homer Phillips*

❖ It's the good girls who keep diaries—bad girls never have time. – *Tallulah Bankhead*

❖ Things of beauty often shake up men who view them minus makeup. – *Ida M. Pardue*

❖ A woman is a person who will spend $20 on a beautiful slip and then be annoyed if it shows. – *D. S. Halacy*

❖ In a hosiery store: "Your face is your fortune, but your legs draw interest." – *Evening news, London*

❖ Two reasons why women don't wear last year's gowns: They don't want to, and they can't.

❖ Glamour gal: sight to be held. – *K-Lens-M Komments*

❖ The talk that occurs as she strolls down the beach shows clearly that hers is a figure of speech. – *Irene Warsaw*

❖ Your dresses should be tight enough to show you're a woman and loose enough to show you're a lady.
– *Edith Head, Hollywood fashion designer*

❖ Gold digger: a woman after all. – *Phoenix Flame*

❖ She lets her mind go blank, but forgets to turn off the sound.
– *Home Life*

❖ Beauty parlor: where the women get a face full of mud and an earful of dirt. – *Nick Kenny*

❖ Gals unhappy about their figures delight in meeting some dame bigger. – *K-Lens-M Komments* (October, 1965)

❖ Women are unpredictable. You never know how they are going to manage to get their own way. – *Franklin P. Jones*

❖ A woman's club is a place where they knock after they enter.

❖ All a woman needs to be successful are two good lines—one a man can listen to and one he can look at. – *Richard Hayes*

Surprising Facts by K-Lens-M Komments

- ❖ Women's spike heels exert 22,000 pounds of pressure per square inch, creating some of the greatest damage to airplane interiors. (Sept., 1963)
- ❖ Brassieres were used 5,000 years ago. (March, 1964)

Work

- Work is the yeast that raises the dough. – *The Irish Digest*

- Be thankful if your job is a little harder than you like. A razor cannot be sharpened on a piece of velvet.

- Uneasy lies the head that tries to make a living without working for it.

- The trouble with soft jobs is they're so hard to hold.

- If you want to kill an idea, just get a committee to work on it.

- Nothing is really work unless you would rather be doing something else.

- During the coffee break, you can always pick out which one is the boss. He is the one watching the clock.

- Anyone can do any amount of work, provided it isn't the work he is supposed to be doing. – *Robert Benchley*

- The nearest to perfection most people ever come is when f illing out an employment application. – *Ken Kraft*

- Some people are so busy learning the tricks of the trade that they don't learn the trade.

- Texas nursery rhyme: "The butcher, the baker, the Cadillac maker." – *H. Lewis*

❖ A man should raise the standard of his work if he is working for a raise.

❖ Man is that foolish creature who shortens his life by working so hard to acquire things that further shorten his life.

❖ Slogan: good old American substitute for the facts.
– *Jacob M. Braude*

❖ There is no future in any job. The future is in the one who holds the job.

❖ If all the businessmen who sleep at their desks were laid end to end they would be more comfortable.

❖ All play and no work takes Jack. – *K-Lens-M Komments*
(August, 1964)

❖ Expert: one who has a good reason for guessing wrong.
– *Walter Winchell*

❖ A man who is pulling his own weight never has any left over to throw around. – *A. A. Battista*

❖ Executive: a man who goes from his air-conditioned office, in an air-conditioned car, to his air-conditioned club, to take a steam bath.

❖ He who thinks he is a big gun finds out how small his caliber is when he is fired.

❖ About ten percent of the people do the world's thinking, so we're told. Judging by the results, we believe half of them would do more good by going to work.

❖ The easiest way to make ends meet is to get off your own.

❖ If you are a self-starter, your boss doesn't have to be a crank.
– *Buck Herzog in Milwaukee Sentinel*

❖ Old salesmen never die. They just get out of commission.

❖ A decision is what a man makes when he can't find anybody to serve on a committee. – *Fletcher Knebel*

❖ Man is the animal that intends to shoot himself out into interplanetary space, after having given up on the problem of an efficient way to get himself five miles or so to work and back each day. – *Bill Vaughan*

❖ A horse must be "broke" before he will work. The same is true of a lot of men.

❖ Too many people judge right from wrong on the basis of which pays the best.

❖ Advertising man: "Yessir, Nosir, Ulcer." – *Lee H. Bristol*

❖ The two most difficult careers are entrusted to amateurs— citizenship and parenthood. – *St. John's, Newfoundland, Herald*

❖ Today's biggest problem is working out solutions for the solutions the last generation worked out. – *Dan Bennett*

❖ Watch out for ambition; it can get you into a lot of work!
– *K-Lens-M Komments* (September, 1963)

❖ It is impossible to hold down a good job unless you stay on it.

❖ Being a telephone girl isn't a business or profession; it's a calling.

❖ He who is full of schemes to make easy money seldom has time for work.

- ❖ He who would eat the kernel must crack the shell.

- ❖ They now have coffee dispensers for office use that look exactly like filing cabinets. These will match up with lots of coffee drinkers who look exactly like office workers. – *H. C. Diefenbach*

- ❖ A conference is a meeting where people talk about what they should already be doing.

- ❖ A psychiatrist claims frustration is responsible for most headaches. The penalty for aspiration is aspirin. – *K-Lens-M Komments* (June, 1962)

- ❖ The owner of a racetrack earns his daily bread by the sweat of some other fellow's brow.

- ❖ It is a tough world for the American businessman. Each time he comes up with something new, the Russians invented it a week earlier and the Japanese make it cheaper.

- ❖ Service while you wait is usually what the other fellow is getting. – *Vesta M. Kelly*

- ❖ Some men remind us of blisters; they don't show up until the work is done. – *Paul Carruth*

- ❖ Work may not be as hard as it used to be, but it is more taxing.

- ❖ Men who claim that the boss is dumb would be out of a job if he were any smarter.

- ❖ Panelist: someone with an ability to think on his seat. – *Bill Cullen*

- ❖ Sales manager: a man who earns his living by being a slave to conventions. – *Ed Wittaker*

❖ If it can be said of your work that not even a competitor can find fault, you know it's good.

❖ An expert in economics is a man who knows tomorrow why the things he said yesterday didn't happen today.

❖ Scientists are predicting a workless world. How about a taxless one? – *K-Lens-M Komments* (May, 1963)

❖ It's a wise man who knows his own business, and it's a wiser one who thoroughly attends to it.

❖ More men are killed by overwork than the importance of the work justifies. – *Rudyard Kipling*

❖ People who do their work well and make good are never asked for explanations.

❖ Don't entertain ideas; put them to work. – *K-Lens-M Komments*

❖ The difference between a junior and senior executive may be as much as 40 pounds. – *Kenneth J. Shively*

❖ Business is like a bicycle. You have to keep it moving forward at a fairly good speed or it starts to wobble.

❖ Recession: your neighbor is out of work. Depression: you are out of work.

❖ Anybody can take a day off, but who can put one back?

❖ The best business to be in is some other. – *K-Lens-M Komments*

❖ More and more people are wanting less to do, with more time to do it in, and more pay for half doing it. Therefore, we have strikes.

❖ There are three times in his life when a man should do his best: yesterday, today, and tomorrow.

❖ When some people find a job, they stop looking for work.

❖ An executive is a person who can take two hours for lunch without having anybody miss him. – *Herbert V. Prochno*

❖ The best way to get a job done is to give it to a busy man. He'll have his secretary do it.

❖ It isn't hard to pull a load downhill. – *K-Lens-M Komments* (August, 1965)

❖ Satisfied customers are an ace in the hole in any business.

❖ He who would have what he hath not should do what he doeth not.

❖ Winter is that season when it is too cold to do the work it was too hot to do last summer.

❖ The hardest thing about business is minding your own.

❖ The severest loyalty test is laughing at the boss's jokes. – *K-Lens-M Komments* (March, 1964)

❖ When a man is enthusiastic about hard work, chances are that he is an employer.

❖ Filing cabinets are repositories where things get lost alphabetically.

❖ Hard work may be highly respectable, but just try and make it popular.

❖ A committee of one gets things done. – *Joe Ryan*

❖ Some guys have more grass growing under their feet than they have on their head. – *K-Lens-M Komments* (August, 1964)

❖ Many a man looks for opportunity with one eye and tries to dodge work at the same time.

❖ Accustomed as I am to public speaking, I know the futility of it.

❖ Some men never try working for a living until they have given everything else a fair trial.

❖ There are 40,000 different ways to earn a living and yours is the hardest. – *K-Lens-M Komments* (March, 1964)

❖ A man must keep a little back shop where he can be himself without reserve. In solitude alone can he know true freedom. – *Montaigne*

❖ A chronic kicker kicks himself out of many good jobs.

❖ What is worrying most employers today is the number of unemployed people on the payroll.

❖ Others can knock free enterprise, but they can't beat it. – *K-Lens-M Komments* (October, 1963)

❖ If something goes wrong, it is more important to talk about who is going to fix it than who is to blame.

❖ It takes more than shouts to make an echo in the business world.

❖ If you would fight competition successfully, mind your own business.

Work

❖ No man works harder against his own interests than he who works for them exclusively.

❖ Commenting on conferences: God needed only six days to create the world, but He had the advantage of working alone.
– *Switzerland's Journal de Geneve*

❖ Nothing is so embarrassing as to watch the boss do something you told him couldn't be done.

❖ Convention: where people pass a lot of resolutions but few bars.
– *Hal Cochran*

❖ Leisure: the time you spend on jobs you don't get paid for.
– *The Changing Times, The Kiplinger Magazine*

❖ Ambition is a fine thing but it sure gets a fellow into a lot of work.

❖ Genius is the ability to evade work by doing something right the first time.

❖ Nothing is so blind as an investigating committee that doesn't want to investigate.

❖ Nice thing about keeping quiet in a meeting is that you'll most likely not be picked to head a committee.

❖ Committee: a group of the unfit, appointed by the unwilling, to do the unnecessary. – *Victor Riesel*

❖ Conference: a meeting of the bored. – *Russell Newbold*

❖ In planning a career, pick work you like and for which you have an ability.

❖ The nice thing about dictating letters is that you can use a lot of words you don't know how to spell.

❖ A good way to keep cool is to work fast enough to start a breeze.

❖ The fellow who never expects to give others a square deal always acts surprised when he comes out on the short end.

❖ An executive is the guy who entertains all the visitors while the other people in the office work.

❖ When a fellow gets to thinking he is a big gun, somebody fires him.

❖ An executive who is always busy is usually doing a lot of stuff an assistant could do twice as well in half the time.

❖ Efficiency expert: a man who walks in his sleep so that he can get his rest and his exercise at the same time.

❖ One never knows how fast he can go until his career starts on a downward course.

❖ What you seem to be may get you a job. What you are may let you keep it.

❖ Coffee break: secretarrying – *Sara Shook*

❖ How nice it would be if all those looking for positions were looking for work.

❖ Make your job important and it will return the favor.

❖ There's a lot to learn from the calendar. It plans its work a year ahead, never complains, always finishes on time, and you don't have to wind it up! – *K-Lens-M Komments*

❖ If lawyers are disbarred and ministers unfrocked, perhaps electricians get delighted, Far East diplomats disoriented, cashiers distilled, alpine climbers dismounted, piano tuners unstrung, orchestra leaders disbanded, artists' models deposed, cooks deranged, nudists redressed, office clerks defiled, mediums dispirited, dressmakers unbiased. – *Marian Forer*

Surprising Facts by K-Lens-M Komments

✓ About 20,000,000 U.S. men attend a total of about 75,000 business conventions a year. (August, 1963)

Worth

- ❖ The world takes you at your worth; it's up to you to establish it.

- ❖ You came into this world not because you chose to—or where you chose to—but because the world had need of you.

- ❖ The information you get from the man who is easy to pump is worthless.

- ❖ Never try to judge a man's worth by the size of his bluff.

- ❖ Taxes could be a lot worse. Suppose we had to pay a tax on what we think we're worth?

Nancy Jones Stroupe

Nancy Lucille Jones Stroupe was born in 1912 in the tiny South Carolina town of Wagener in Aiken County near Columbia. She was the oldest of "the four Jones girls," as they were called by friends of the family.

Their father, Oscar Jones, was a master painter whose handiwork can still be seen in the old homes in the area. He was also a prolific fisherman who, although he had no son to follow in his footsteps, loved to take his girls fishing. Their mother, Eva Madora Jeanette Antoinette Brown Jones, spent much of her time during the week in Columbia managing the interior-decorating department of a large department store.

Mrs. Stroupe decided in the third grade that she wanted to be a teacher and, once her course was set, she never doubted or rethought her decision. She felt she was born to teach and her passion for the English language and world literature made her choice of subjects easy. She loved to study how words evolved and she included Latin in her subjects to teach.

In 1931, she moved to the mountains of North Carolina and launched her dream in pedagogy. In 1935, she married Odes Stroupe, whose large and closely-knit family had moved to the mountains from Cherryville, N.C. in 1912.

Mr. Stroupe had taught school, had been a school principal as were his brothers Rush and Lee, and then was offered a job as district manager for Nationwide Insurance (then Farm Bureau) in Charlotte, N.C. After several years away from Avery County and after the births of their two children, the Stroupes returned to their loving home and never left again except for winters in Florida after they both retired.

Nancy Stroupe Morrison

Nancy Stroupe Morrison grew up in the North Carolina High Country. Her mother taught English and Latin. Her father was Nationwide Insurance Company's first field underwriter. She graduated from Newland High School, where she was valedictorian of her class, head cheerleader, and editor-in-chief/business manager of her high school yearbook. She graduated from St. Andrews University with a degree in psychology and sociology and did her graduate work at the University of North Carolina at Chapel Hill. She was a social worker with Scotland County DSS, a counselor in mental health in Robeson County, senior therapist at the Alcoholic Rehabilitation Center in Butner, North Carolina, and was director of therapeutic services and director of the long-term care unit at the Charlotte Detox. She also owned Goodman Entertainment & Events in Charlotte and booked musical entertainment on the east coast for many years. She moved to Avery County in 1994 to care for her ailing father. She became manager for the Avery Mountain Times and then publisher/editor for the Avery Journal-Times and All About Women magazine. When she retired from publishing, she reinvented herself as an artist in a field she always loved.

Mrs. Morrison has served on and headed dozens of boards in Avery County. She also organized a six-month campaign and established two K-9 units for the Avery County Sheriff's Office; she worked with the SBI, local law enforcement and the NC Attorney General's Office to rid Avery County of local governmental corruption; was instrumental in passing the "No Felon For Sheriff" statute in N.C.; spearheaded efforts that obtained drug treatment court for Avery and Watauga counties; was elected to the Hall of Legends in 2015; was voted Woman of the Year in 2013; received Outstanding Service Award from Chamber of Commerce in 2010; received the Distinguished Service Award from Mayland Community College in 2008, and has won numerous awards from the N.C. Press Association, including Best Column, Investigative Reporting, and Community Service.

Danica De La Mora

For more than a decade, Danica De La Mora has been following a plant-based lifestyle, building on her collection of knowledge through extensive study and education lectures by doctors who are at the forefront of the latest in nutritional research. She is a graduate of the Plant-Based Nutrition program by the Center for Nutrition Studies at Cornell University under Dr. T. Colin Campbell, Dr. Thomas M. Campbell, Dr. Dean Ornish, Dr. Caldwell Esselstyn, and other professionals.

She also holds a degree in Communication and Film Studies from St. Andrews University and is a graduate of the Barbizon modeling academy. She has a background in graphic design, multiple forms of editing, DVD authoring, film transfer and preservation, videography, photography, and photograph restoration, as well as print media production, having been reared in a family who owned print publications all over the Southeastern United States.

Ms. De La Mora has been strongly influenced by her family. She is experienced in Latin and ballroom dancing, as well as music, with her grandmother's ownership of a prestigious etiquette and dance school for 50 years and her father having placed fourth in the world on accordion out of thousands of contestants. In addition to her own research and experience with relationships, she has obtained substantial knowledge through her mother's wide-ranging background involving social work, alcoholism treatment, psychology, and print media publishing. Her grandparents' loving and traditional marriage of nearly 60 years provided her with an excellent foundation for understanding successful relationships and gender polarities.

Ms. De La Mora advises groups and individuals of all ages who are interested in refining themselves with a traditional and conservative elegance. She leads them down the path of optimal nutrition so that they may regain health, prevent disease, and enjoy long-term weight management. She also counsels ladies and gentlemen in their romantic relationships and helps them find the fulfilling lives that they were destined to enjoy.

From the manner in which one conducts oneself to the manner in which one presents oneself, elegance is everything!

Ms. De La Mora is happy to help anyone who has the desire for improvement in personal refinement, etiquette, manners, nutrition, or romance. Feel free to send her an email: info@DanicaDeLaMora.com

www.DanicaDeLaMora.com
blog.DanicaDeLaMora.com
Gab & Twitter: @DanicaDeLaMora

TIMELESS
TREASURES
PUBLISHING

A Timeless Treasures Publication.

www.ingramcontent.com/pod-product-compliance
Lightning Source LLC
Chambersburg PA
CBHW020654270326
41928CB00005B/121